Things That Work

SAIL's
Things That Work

International Marine
Camden, Maine

To sailors everywhere who work on their boats,
especially those who have contributed ideas to
SAIL's "Things That Work" column—
this book is for you.

Published by International Marine

10 9 8 7 6 5 4 3 2

Copyright ©1994 SAIL Magazine

All rights reserved. The publisher takes no responsibility for the use of any of the materials or methods described in this book, nor for the products thereof. The name "International Marine" and the International Marine logo are trademarks of McGraw-Hill, Inc. Printed in the United States of America.

Library of Congress Cataloging-in-Publication Data
SAIL's Things that work.
   p. cm.
   Hints and mini-projects contributed by the readers of *SAIL*.
   Includes index.
   ISBN 0-87742-374-1
   1. Sailboats--Equipment and supplies. I. Sail. II. Title:
Things that work.
VM351.S244 1993
623.8'223'028--dc20   93-36351
                                  CIP

Questions regarding the content of this book should be addressed to:

International Marine
P.O. Box 220
Camden, ME 04843

Questions regarding the ordering of this book should be addressed to:

TAB Books
A Division of McGraw-Hill, Inc.
Blue Ridge Summit, PA 17294
1-800-233-1128

SAIL's *Things That Work* is printed on 60-pound Renew Opaque Vellum, an acid-free paper which contains 50 percent recycled waste paper (preconsumer) and 10 percent postconsumer waste paper.

Printed by R.R. Donnelley, Harrisonburg, VA
Design by Faith Hague
Production by Dan Kirchoff

Contents

Sailing Made More Fun *61*

Index   *81*

Introduction

I'm pleased to present these ideas on how to make sailing your cruising boat easier, safer, and more fun. The hints and mini-projects here were contributed by readers of *SAIL*, who have tested them for at least a year aboard their own boats. They were selected by *SAIL*'s editors and by Lin and Larry Pardey and Ralph and Leonore Naranjo, who are *SAIL* contributors and experienced cruisers.

A few years ago, in *SAIL*'s offices, we had a long session with Lin and Larry during which we kicked ideas around. We discussed the fact that many of the bluewater cruising boats that passed through New Zealand (where the Pardeys were living and getting ready to go voyaging again) had been customized in small ways by their owners. These "little ideas" could prove useful to other cruisers—many of whom, after sailing, are second-happiest tinkering—if there were a way to bring these ideas to them. Thus, "Things That Work," the magazine column, was born. Now as you leaf through the pages of this book, think of it as a branch on the nautical grapevine—presented in the same spirit in which sailors pass along ideas in a boatyard, marina, or anchorage.

As we were preparing the material for this book, I was struck by a number of things. First is the pride of ownership contributors show for their boats and their enthusiasm for sailing. In the letters presenting their suggestions for "Things That Work," sailors also eagerly describe their vessels and their cruising, both near and far. Contributors hail from more than two dozen U.S. states and Canadian provinces and from several foreign countries. They sail close to home and far away. Their ideas are a collective portrait of how we all cruise.

The second thing that struck me is the ingenuity of cruisers. Often a sailor has simply discovered a new use for an ordinary object, such as Californian Jason Halley's using a hot-water bottle to add oil to his inaccessible engine, and Massachusetts sailor Bob Whittier's idea for using a chalkboard eraser as a sandpaper block because its flexible shape conforms to difficult contours. Other ideas are in the dead-simple, why-didn't-I-think-of-that category: using white vinegar to clean up uncured resin, discovered by Ontario cruiser Peter Martyn, or using fingernail polish for color-coded, watertight seals on electrical connections, a trick employed by Charles Squires of Virginia. Still others involve clever techniques, such as the method invented by Harvey Wallace of California for folding the jib on the small foredeck of his 27-footer.

Third, these are grassroots ideas. In most cases they come from owners of boats between 20 and 35 feet long. None costs a great deal to implement, but they give a customized feel to each boat. Even ideas that involve construction or installation don't require a master mechanic or carpenter. Witness Californian Jane Piereth's simple suggestion for attaching a row of teak drink holders to a board cut to fit the bottom of the companionway opening.

We don't exactly know why the owners of small- to medium-size boats seem to be tinkerers and inventors. Clearly, the reason for some is economics; but we think it's also type. Sailors willing to take the risks involved in cruising are willing to chance a new idea. Most projects on boats this size are pretty basic. A word of caution, however. Before you try any of these ideas, make sure the engineering is correct for your size boat. If you have a 35-footer and the "Things That Work" project is for a 22-footer, it's best to seek expert advice before you begin.

We've had our Skye 51, *Boston Light*, for 10 years, including a 22-month circumnavigation. You would think that by now the urge and need to personalize and tinker would be dormant. Far from it! In the past year we have redesigned the lazyjack system for our mainsail and found that a small PVC pipe lashed vertically to the forwardmost stanchion keeps our windlass handle handy and onboard. This is the spirit of "Things

That Work"—not an addiction to alteration that keeps you at the dock, but a desire to make changes that allow you to entertain in the cockpit, organize stowage so you can find things in emergencies, and add some simple hardware so you can trim your sails more efficiently.

I ask just one favor. If you like the way one or more of these ideas works on your boat, pass it on to your sailing friends. We'd like to keep the grapevine growing.

Patience Wales

Editor, *SAIL*
August 1993

Sailing Made Easier

*T*HE BETTER MOUSETRAP. Most of us would love to have a few onboard—to make sailing easier and you and the crew happier. Here's a whole collection of ideas from cruiser-tinkerers, who have done something about the onboard irritations that prevent efficient and really enjoyable sailing.

Retired to his family's hometown on the north coast of Nova Scotia, Willard Boyle cruises a 20-foot, British-built Seadrift, which sits contentedly on its bilge keels in front of Boyle's home at each low tide. Despite the boat's hefty 4,500-pound displacement, Boyle needs to roller-reef the headsail in over 20 knots of wind. For proper headsail trim he needed a genoa track so he could adjust the position of the jibsheet car, but he has little deck space and a disinclination to drill holes. His "mousetrap" is a sort of permanently installed barberhauler, described in this section. With his "amazing little boat" rigged for heavy- and light-air sail trim, Boyle, alone or with one crewmember, has embarked on "some fair expeditions" to Prince Edward Island and the Bras d'Or Lakes.

Like Boyle, Robert Dougherty of Ozona, Florida, proves it's possible to make sailing easier even on pocket cruisers. Dougherty needed a way to transport his outboard motor from his garage to his Santana 21 at the dock behind his home each time he went sailing. A $5 cart from a flea market with some minor alterations puts him on the water for daysails more easily and more often.

When he used to bring his S2 11.0C back to the dock, Carl Wohltmann of Danville, California, a 20-year veteran of sailing Lake Ontario and San Francisco Bay, was tired of saying to his crew: "Pull this dockline, release that one . . ." until the boat was centered, not touching either side of the slip. Then he got the idea of marking his docklines, first with indelible ink, later with color-coded whippings. Ending a sail became much less of a hassle. That problem solved, Wohltmann went on to discover a way to mount his hand-held VHF in a waterproof plastic bag in the cockpit and to invent a foolproof method for remembering to open the seacock to cool the engine each time before leaving the dock.

In today's world, making things easier usually implies making them move faster—sending messages electronically instead of by mail, driving faster on a new highway, being bombarded by eye-blink-fast television images. In this section of *SAIL'S Things That Work*, "easier" does mean the efficiency available in modern life with modern materials, but not necessarily at modern pace. After all, for many of us sailing is our escape, our way of stopping the world and floating away. First and foremost, easier means more enjoyable.

A Modern Monkey Fist

From Tony Hunter of Corpus Christi, Texas, comes an idea for a convenient heaving line. He writes: "For the past couple of years I have been using a softball to replace the sailor's traditional monkey fist. Because the softball has a cork interior, it floats and does not become waterlogged. I used an awl, marine twine, and a sail needle to stitch a piece of leather to the ball cover; it forms a strap long enough that a piece of ¼-inch line can be secured to the ball. I form this line into a small loop." Then Hunter uses a bowline to secure a slightly larger (⅜-inch-diameter) heaving line to the monkey fist. His estimate of three times the length of the boat as an adequate heaving line seems about right. He recommends tying a large loop so the line can be dropped over a convenient bollard.

Hunter continues, "For throwing, hold three loose coils of the heaving line plus the softball in your throwing hand; coil the rest of the line loosely and hold it in the other hand. Throw the softball underhanded to carry the line toward shore. Since most people are familiar with a softball, they will not be intimidated by seeing one flying in their direction. This should help them to catch it and the line. If the heaving line is to be thrown on board another boat, there is little chance of the softball doing any damage to that boat or to its crew."

Lin and Larry Pardey, too, have used a heaving line to help other people guide their boat into a Mediterranean mooring situation and agree with Tony that one should be kept handy in a cockpit locker. Theirs is stored with the line coiled inside a canvas bag and the monkey fist outside, ready to grab in a hurry.

Dockline Saver

Vern Barkel of Holland, Michigan, has discovered a way to keep docklines from fraying before their time. He has been tying up to 4-inch diameter steel pilings for the past few years, causing fraying to be more rapid than on less abrasive wooden pilings.

His solution begins with cutting the top and bottom off polyvinyl-chloride plastic bottles (bleach and milk), slitting the tube-like leftover portion, and wiring or tying with twine this slippery bearing-like device around the piling. A dockline's sliding and jerking on these piling covers endures a fraction of the abrasion associated with the uncovered piling. A pair of these containers properly lashed together and located will cover a piling up to a foot in diameter. Lines last a lot longer and the nearly indestructible PVC bottles are reused prior to recycling, a cost-effective environmentally sound endeavor.

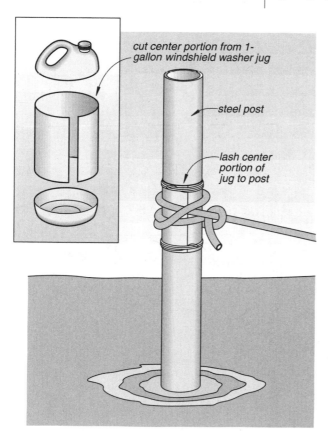

cut center portion from 1-gallon windshield washer jug

steel post

lash center portion of jug to post

Backing in Safely

When singlehanding his Seaward 24, William A. Gannon of Audubon, New Jersey, found he needed a way to back into his slip against strong cross currents.

He rigged permanent lines (made up of spliced-together odd pieces of old rope) that go from the pilings on the exit end of his slip to the floating dock (finger pier). He spliced a snap-eye onto another old line. He then took the snap-eye and ran it through a fairlead on the bow, bringing it back along the outside of his lifelines to the cockpit.

As he begins to back into his slip, he snaps the eye onto the line near the piling that is upwind or up-current. Then, as he backs in, he pulls the other end of the line to keep the bow from falling off, controlling the bow as he works the stern toward the floating dock.

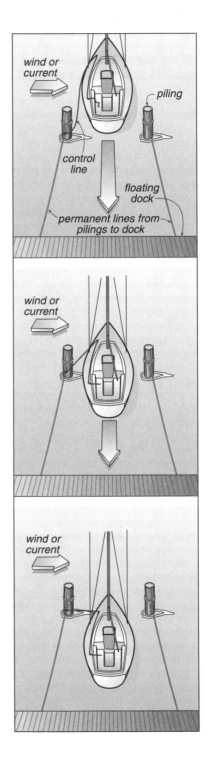

Position Marks on Lines

"We like to see our 11-meter S2 sloop, *Prosperity*, tied exactly in the center of her slip. To cut down on the readjustments we once had to make, we have marked the dock lines with whippings where the line touches the cleat," writes Carl A. Wohltmann of Danville, California. "It is a simple matter to cleat each line at its mark, knowing that a perfect position is guaranteed when all the lines are tied. The marks can also be made with permanent marker. Either way, they do not affect the use of the dock lines when you are tying up at other docks."

On board their 30-foot wooden cutter *Taleisin* Larry and Lin Pardey have used whipping markers such as these to indicate the correct positioning of the spinnaker-pole topping lift and the preferred lazyjack position. Nylon whipping thread can be felt at night and has lasted several years, so it is their first choice.

Cut-the-Shouting Headset

Bill Dabbs of Torrance, California, writes: "Kathy and I spend as many weekends as possible cruising the Channel Islands of Southern California on our Crealock 34 cutter, *Sea Dabb's*. We generally leave after work on Friday evenings, so we arrive at crowded anchorages late at night. We had problems picking our way through moorings, anchor lines, and tied-off dinghies to anchor or pick up a mooring, especially when there was no moon. We didn't want to wake people by shouting instructions, and hand signals couldn't be seen.

"We solved the problem by using a toy called My First Sony. This voice-activated transmitter/receiver headset has more than sufficient range to cover the distance between the bow and helm. It leaves both hands free to handle the windlass or helm. Instructions can be given in a normal voice regardless of wind or engine noise. The plastic housing is very sturdy, and we are still on the first set of 9-volt batteries.

"Although we look a little strange with our 'Enterprise' headsets, we have not had one husband-and-wife anchoring spat in almost two years of use."

5

Building a Fender Board

Craig Holmes of Yarmouth Port, Massachusetts, offers instructions for a fender board that you can build for under $10. Just follow these simple steps.

1. The length of the board you will need depends on the curve of the hull and the diameter of the fenders. The sharper the hull curve and the thinner the fenders, the shorter the board must be. Holmes used a 5-foot, 6-inch piece of 2x4 for his fender board and secured it to 8-inch-by-23-inch fenders.

2. For the support lines, drill two ⅜-inch holes through the 4-inch width of the board, one approximately 6 inches from each end.

3. To make the lines that will support the fender board, you'll need two pieces of ⁵⁄₁₆-inch line approximately 15 inches long; weave an eyesplice at one end of each. Feed the unspliced ends through the holes you've just drilled, and tie a stopper knot at the end (see figure).

4. Drill two ⅜-inch holes through the board the short way on either side of the support line at each end. The two holes at each end of the board should be 2 inches closer together than the fender diameter.

5. Widen all four holes on one side of the board with a ⅝-inch bit to a depth of about ⅝ inch—enough to allow a knot to be countersunk flush with the face of the board.

6. Cut two pieces of shock cord approximately 3 inches shorter than the circumference of the fenders. Thread the lines through the two pairs of holes from the back side of the board and tie knots at the ends. Recess these knots into the countersunk holes (see inset).

7. Hang the board on the outside of two fenders by sliding the support-line eyesplices over the fender lines. Stretch one shock cord loop around each fender. The board will remain secure on the fenders, and you can adjust it for dock height.

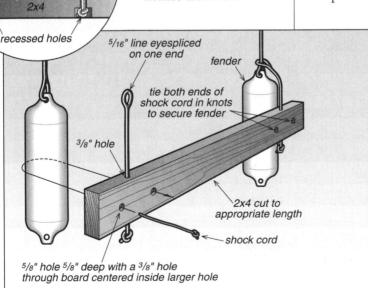

fender

shock cord

2x4

recessed holes

⁵⁄₁₆" line eyespliced on one end

fender

tie both ends of shock cord in knots to secure fender

⅜" hole

2x4 cut to appropriate length

shock cord

⅝" hole ⅝" deep with a ⅜" hole through board centered inside larger hole

Dinghy Bumpers

David Buckman of Gilford, New Hampshire, has found a do-it-yourself alternative to costly dinghy fender material.

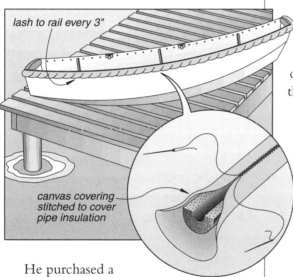

lash to rail every 3"

canvas covering stitched to cover pipe insulation

He purchased a package of ½-inch foam pipe insulation (the non-water-absorbing, closed-cell variety) and two yards of white canvas; the total cost was $19.

He writes: "I sliced the pipe insulation in half (it was already slit on one side) and cut a length of canvas wide enough to wrap around the foam and allow the cut edge of the fabric to be tucked under, to eliminate exposed-edge fraying." Then with a needle in hand and a double line of polyester thread, he spent two hours sewing it together. He taped the foam together and, when he came to the end of the first six foot length of canvas covering, he overlapped the next length a couple of inches and sewed them together.

Running a steam iron over the back seam when it was finished snugged the canvas up nicely. All that remained was to lace it to the gunwale of the dinghy (at 3-inch intervals) with whipping twine.

Buckman writes, "It looks good and because this foam is a bit softer than the store-bought stuff, it works better too." He says he's got enough canvas left over to re-cover the bumpers three or four times.

Dinghy Control

Tom Tursi of Horsham, Pennsylvania, finds his dinghy has a mind of its own. "No matter what I want it to do, it always does the opposite, and when I think it's going to do the opposite, it finds something else to do." His solution is simplicity itself: Use a double painter, one secured to each stern cleat, run it through the dinghy's bow ring, and adjust the length depending on the situation.

When under sail, allow a generous length of painter for trailing a hard dinghy. You'll find that the dinghy trails better with two painters, not to mention the added security of having an extra line. When you're docking or anchored for the night, the inflatable dinghy can be snugged in tight to the transom with both painters. If you lift the bow against the transom and tie it off, your inflatable will ride quietly through the night.

Eliminate Black Marks

The little rubber tips on inflatables often leave black marks not only on the topside of the owner's boat, but also on the topsides of boats he visits. Dave Nof of Saint Petersburg, Florida, solved this problem: "Grind down the tips of the dinghy to a somewhat smooth finish (I used a belt sander). Be careful not to touch the main tubes while you are grinding. Clean the area and apply adhesive from your inflatable patching kit. Cut some material just a bit larger than needed and follow the directions for patching a hole. The next day trim excess material off the cover-up patch and clean excess glue off the tubes with acetone. These patches will relieve you from the job of scrubbing black marks from your sailboat's hull."

Lin and Larry add, "As our boat receives these black marks, as well as scratches from inflatables caused when the rings along the outside hit our hull paint, we wonder if the same idea couldn't be adapted to cover the rings."

Nonmarking Dinghy Paint

Herb Payson writes: "If you are someone whose inflatable dinghy endears you to your fussy friends by leaving black marks all over their topsides, there is an answer." Herb says that Marine Development and Research (MDR) of Merrick, New York, makes a thick white vinyl paint for anchor chain. Friends aboard *Rafiki* in Great Cruz Bay, St. John, in the U.S. Virgin Islands, painted the rubstrake and handles (which also protrude) on their inflatable with this anchor chain paint, and after a year the paint shows no sign of rubbing off. Herb comments, "Recently we, too, painted our blackmark-making jewel, and friends we thought we had lost have resumed inviting us over."

Payson suggests the following steps: Wash the parts to be painted with fresh water. Sand with coarse (80 grit) sandpaper, making sure all surfaces are thoroughly scuffed. Rinse liberally with acetone. Tape and paint three coats, allowing an hour drying time between coats, and 24 hours before use. The paint dries fast, so you must try to avoid rebrushing.

The paint can be thinned with MDR 170 thinner or methylethyl ketone. Acetone works too, but not nearly as well.

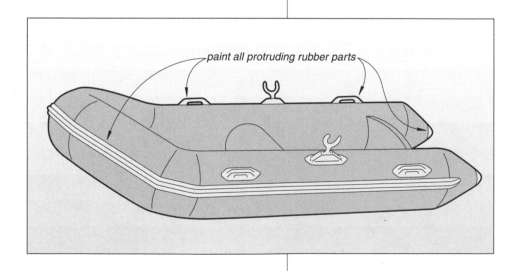

paint all protruding rubber parts

Centerboard Pusher

Centerboards have been known to become stuck in the raised position at the most inopportune times. All it takes is some sand or barnacles to jam the board inside the slot.

Boat designer Roberto Hosmann of Buenos Aires, Argentina, has come up with an effective solution to the problem. His sketches detail a centerboard-pushing mechanism that can be retrofitted to many centerboard-trunk designs. Once installed, a threaded plug caps the tube

and can be quickly replaced with a push rod when it's time to free a stuck centerboard. It takes just a few turns of the screw-driven rod to get rid of a problem that might otherwise spoil a cruise.

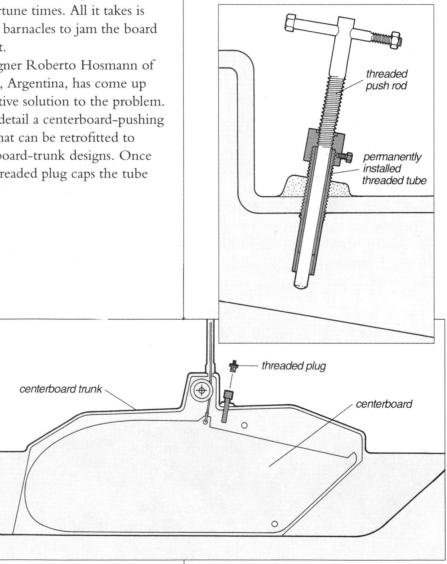

threaded push rod

permanently installed threaded tube

threaded plug

centerboard trunk

centerboard

Adjustable Tie-Downs

Orin Main of Fernandina Beach, Florida, got tired of never having the right length of spare line around for tying this or that aboard his 50-foot Alden ketch, *Tahoma*. He cut line in 6-foot lengths and spliced eyes at each end. The lines can be easily coupled together to provide line of any length. The line-assembly procedure is simple. Take the eyesplice of one line and slip it through the eyesplice of a second line. Then pass the entire length of the first line through its own eyesplice and tighten. Repeat these steps for each segment added. The line can be quickly adjusted to any length, and the splicing, says Main, is a great winter project.

Custom Stanchion Fittings

Tom Flader of Fond du Lac, Wisconsin, has made a variety of useful devices from PVC tubing that has the same inside diameter as the outside diameter of his stanchions and pulpits. He cuts and removes a lengthwise slit from the tubing so he can snap the remaining portion of the tubing securely onto a stanchion or pulpit. The greater the width of the removed slice, the easier it is to snap the tubing on and off the stanchion. Flader has found that starting with a small slice and then gradually filing away the edges with a file or plane makes it easier to adjust the tubing's holding power.

These fittings can secure many things to your boat on a temporary "light load" basis. With countersunk screws driven from the inside out through the tubing's centerline you can screw to the tubing whatever you want to secure to the stanchions or pulpits, such as small cleats for fenders, a flagstaff, a temporary antenna, a flashlight holder, etc.

Solar-Panel Mount

Conrad and Charlotte Skladal of Sunnyvale, California, who sailed to East Africa on *Wisp*, found a place to mount a solar panel that is not only out of the way but is well placed to catch the sun's rays.

They replaced the top lifeline wire between the aft lifeline stanchion and the stern pulpit with a 1-inch-diameter stainless-steel tube. To attach the tube, a hole the size of the stanchion post was drilled in one end so it slipped over the stanchion. It was then secured with a clevis pin. The other end of the tube was notched to slide over the part of the stern pulpit that secured the original lifeline.

A clevis pin also secured this connection. The solar panel was then mounted on a piece of ½-inch plywood (check your solar panel owner's manual for mounting instructions) that had the ends angled as shown. Two U-bolts were used to clamp the plywood board to the stainless-steel tube. The use of a wing nut and a lock nut on each bolt allowed the clamps to be eased off so that the panel could be rotated to face the sun.

To lead the wire from the panel to the house batteries, the Skladals used a short conduit of ½-inch copper tube that leads to a ⅜-inch pipe-compression fitting. The pipe fitting is tapped into the fiberglass deck and installed with silicone sealant to make an inexpensive, waterproof through-deck installation.

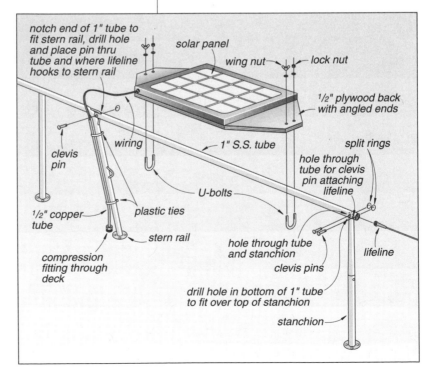

notch end of 1" tube to fit stern rail, drill hole and place pin thru tube and where lifeline hooks to stern rail

solar panel

wing nut — lock nut

½" plywood back with angled ends

clevis pin

wiring

1" S.S. tube

split rings

hole through tube for clevis pin attaching lifeline

½" copper tube

plastic ties

U-bolts

hole through tube and stanchion

lifeline

stern rail

clevis pins

compression fitting through deck

drill hole in bottom of 1" tube to fit over top of stanchion

stanchion

Genoa-Track Alternative

deficiency was particularly noticeable sailing to windward with the jib partially reefed." Forced to improvise, he installed a turning block on the cabintop and ran a

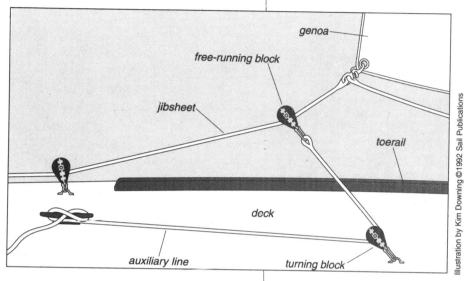

genoa

free-running block

jibsheet

toerail

deck

auxiliary line

turning block

Illustration by Kim Downing © 1992 Sail Publications

When Willard S. Boyle from Wallace, Nova Scotia, tried to install a genoa track on his Seadrift pocket cruiser, he found that there was no space to install it. "The boat came equipped with jib-furling gear, but there was no way to effectively adjust the lead on the jibsheet," he says. "The

line through the block to a free-running block on the jibsheet. The jib can now be closehauled by shortening the auxiliary line to the free-running block. The resulting arrangement allows Boyle to adjust sail shape and keep the jibsheet under control when tacking.

No More Battens Overboard

Tired of losing battens overboard, Patrice Baker of Clifton Park, New York, has discovered another use for Velcro.

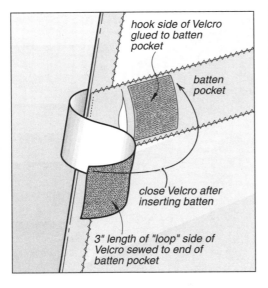

hook side of Velcro glued to batten pocket

batten pocket

close Velcro after inserting batten

3" length of "loop" side of Velcro sewed to end of batten pocket

All too often a batten would manage to shake loose from its pocket, hit the water, and sink out of sight while Baker was reefing, hoisting, or dropping the mainsail. After some research, she purchased a 2-inch-wide strip of Velcro to equal the width of the batten pocket, as well as some Velcro adhesive. She then sewed a 3-inch length of the loop side of the Velcro to the leech of the sail near the end of the batten pocket. Next she glued the hook side of the Velcro, hooks out, to the outside of the batten pocket. The 3-inch tape of Velcro folds over the pocket opening and locks the batten in place.

Outboard Dolly

Robert Dougherty, who sails a "nameless" Santana 21 out of Palm Harbor, Florida, has found an inexpensive way to put wheels on his auxiliary outboard motor. At a flea market he purchased an old hand utility cart for $5. He attached a short piece of 2x4 with U-bolts at the top of the cart to act as the outboard's mounting bracket. When he wants to move his outboard, he simply clamps it down onto the bracket and wheels the motor away.

When he wants to flush out the motor, he slips a 6-gallon plastic bucket (which grocery stores often have) under the propeller while the motor is hanging from the transporter, fills the bucket with fresh water, and starts it up.

The cart also makes a dandy frame on which to store the motor in the garage. After running fresh water through the motor, he wheels it into place and tosses a cover over it.

Reefing Convenience

Steve Christensen of Midland, Michigan, found a way to expedite reefing aboard his Precision 23, *Kittiwake*. The reefing process had required removing a sail stop from the sail-slide groove so that the new tack cringle could be pulled down enough to reach the reefing hook. Not only was the stop difficult to remove at times, but if it wasn't replaced, the mainsail spilled out all over the deck when the halyard was released. He set out to find a better way to reef.

He writes: "I needed a couple of narrow strips to screw over the opening in the sail track after the sail-track slides were inserted that would close off the track so that a sail stop would no longer be necessary. I went to my local ACE Hardware store and found just what I needed: ¾-inch-wide aluminum tile edging, sold in a 36-inch strip for only $2.75. The lip on this edging is about the same thickness as that of the mast track itself, so the mainsail slides don't get hung up as they pass over the strips when the mainsail is raised or lowered.

"I cut two strips just long enough to cover the opening, filed the edges smooth, and fastened them to the mast with machine screws." Don't use self-tapping screws, as you will have to remove these whenever you want to remove the mainsail completely from the mast.

"The result has been great! Not only do I reef more easily and no longer have to mess with the sail stop, but this rig also has the benefit of allowing the main to lie closer to the boom when furled, making it easier to put the mainsail cover on."

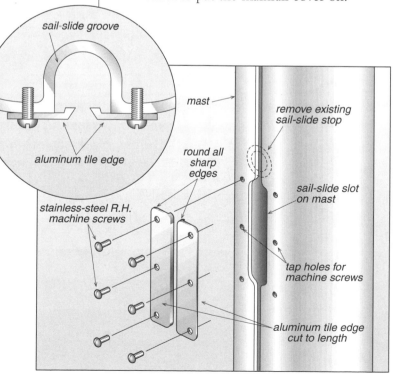

sail-slide groove

aluminum tile edge

mast

remove existing sail-slide stop

round all sharp edges

sail-slide slot on mast

stainless-steel R.H. machine screws

tap holes for machine screws

aluminum tile edge cut to length

Sail Folding Made Simple

Like many people who learn to sail at a school, Harvey Wallace of San Jose, California, was frustrated when the techniques he was taught did not include ways to fold a jib on board so it would fit in the often undersized sail bags supplied by sailmakers. His solution for folding a headsail on the small foredeck of a 27-foot boat is worth sharing, since it can be done at anchor or at sea.

Wallace writes: "Use one sheet to pull the clew back, and fasten it to the mast. If the jib has a longer J measurement [the length of the jib's "bottom," or the length from clew to tack] than the length of the foredeck, you may have to stretch the foot past the mast and attach it temporarily at some other point. I hoist the jib loosely and leave a wrap of the halyard around the winch; then I ease the halyard slowly with one hand while I use my other hand to fold the sail back and forth as it falls

onto the foredeck. If there is a breeze, I use one foot to hold the fold in place while I lower the sail to make the next fold. (Be careful not to put your weight

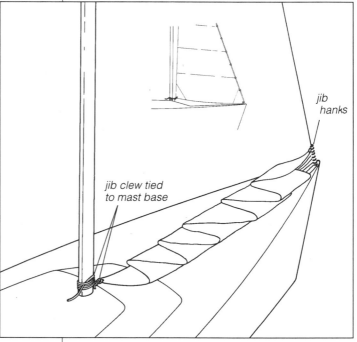

jib hanks

jib clew tied to mast base

on that foot, or you may slip.) Once the entire jib is down and folded from foot to head, I remove all the jib hanks and then fold it from tack to clew. With a little practice, I learned to determine how tightly I needed to fold the jib to get it to fit inside my bag."

Rigid Sail Bags

Martin L. Browne of Brookline, Massachusetts, has a simple way to carefully car-top resinated one-design sails.

Browne states, "When my wife and I bought our Sonar, a 23-foot one-design daysailer, we had a problem fitting the carefully rolled tubes of resinated sails onto our car without bending them."

They bought some bamboo poles, cut them to the appropriate lengths for each rolled sail, and pushed them into the bagged sails for support. Bamboo is cheap, light, and easily cut using a normal wood saw. Martin says, "Our sails can now be tied on top of our car without bending, creasing, or otherwise damaging the finish of the sails or the car."

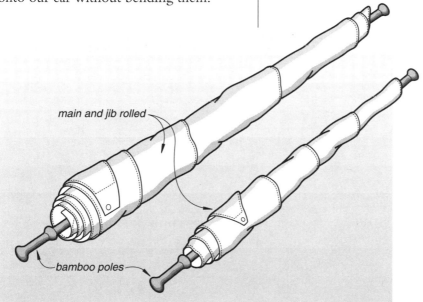

main and jib rolled

bamboo poles

Fluid Control

Kip Bodi of Laurel Hollow, New York, added a sillcock fitting to a plastic bucket to help with winterizing his boat engine and to control the flow of fluids into the engine from the cockpit.

This set-up also solves the problem of trying to get gravity working for you with a siphon and avoids the sloshing of antifreeze and other fluids into the bilge.

He simply attaches a hose to the sillcock and leads the hose down to the engine's raw-water intake hose. Water from a garden hose fills the bucket in the cockpit, overflow exits the cockpit drain, and fresh water flushes the raw-water system.

Once the flushing process is complete, he uses the bucket to add the recommended amount of antifreeze to the heat-exchanger system.

The entire apparatus costs less than $10 to build and Bodi finds it quite useful for winterization and commissioning work. This mechanism can also be used to recapture environmentally destructive antifreeze prior to launching, which can be saved and reused next season.

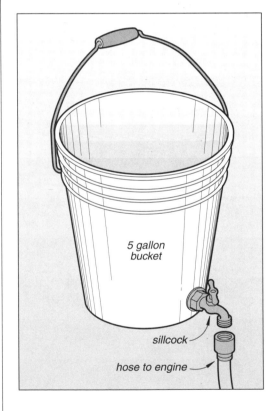

5 gallon bucket

sillcock

hose to engine

Fluid Filler

Jason Halley from Playa Del Rey, California, has found that a hot-water bottle with a hose and a shutoff is the ideal tool for pouring fluids into hard-to-access fillholes. The Perkins 4-107 aboard his boat, *Argo*, is a tight fit, and the very confined space makes pouring oil difficult. He found that using a hot-water bottle permits smooth flow and eliminates mess. The bottle also works to top off transmission fluids, battery water, and coolant reservoirs. Use several hot water bottles for different fluids or clean one bottle thoroughly between uses to avoid mixing fluids.

Fuel-Gauge Alternative

Bill Nichtberger, skipper of the ketch *Cetris,* has an innovative solution for those wondering how much fuel is left in a gaugeless propane or CNG bottle. To check the fuel level, slowly pour hot water down the side of the tank. The hot water causes the top layer of fuel in the tank to change from a liquid to a gas, which in turn causes the surface point of the liquid to become the coolest point on the tank exterior. Run your hand over the side of the tank. A perceptible temperature difference can be felt at the top of the remaining fuel. The hotter the water, the greater the temperature change at the liquid/gas interface.

Drip-Proof Varnish Pot

When you are varnishing or painting, an overloaded brush makes for less-than-perfect finishes. Wiping the brush on the side of the can not only introduces bubbles into the finish, but eventually makes for a messy, sticky can and an overloaded, bubble-laden brush. Wes Golemon of Oxnard, California, describes his perfect varnish can, one with a cut wire for brush wiping, that solves this problem. He uses a small, flat can, like an old-style coffee can, and strings a piece of bailing wire tightly between two holes that he has punched out of either side of the can. The holes are positioned about ¼ inch below the rim and are offset from an imaginary centerline so that the wire will not interfere with dipping the brush. When he is finished varnishing, he rinses the pot just once with thinner and stores it upside-down. It stays clean and will last for years because the residual coating of varnish that is left behind seals the can against rust.

Varnish-Brush Storage

Dan Senecal of Ballston Spa, New York, has a good idea when it comes to applying multiple layers of paint or varnish. "If it's late and you're going to be back at it in the morning, wrap the brushes in foil or a plastic bag and chuck them in the freezer. They'll keep forever, defrost in minutes, and cut cleanup time tremendously."

Varnish-Removal Aid

John Hazen Jr. of *Windward Pilgrim,* Kaneohe Bay, Hawaii, writes: "I am removing a lot of old varnish from the 10-year-old, ill-maintained Flicka I just purchased. I used to be a cabinetmaker and learned to use and appreciate cabinet scrapers. I have been using a cheap and disposable substitute scraper that I buy at the local building-materials outlet. Look for these substitutes in bins labeled 'joist hangers,' 'post-anchors,' 'beam ties,' and the like; I pay about 25 cents for them.

"Simpson Strong Ties are pieces of galvanized sheet metal that are stamped out on a machine. They are drilled and bent into various shapes for connecting framing members in house building. My favorite is a nailing plate, a rectangle about 2 inches by 5 inches, which has several rows of tiny holes drilled through it. The holes aren't important, but the burr that is created when this nailing plate is stamped out is. I choose the ones that have the most pronounced burr around all four edges. I use paint remover, wait 15 minutes, and then go to work with my 25-cent scrapers, throwing them away when they are dull."

The various other Simpson Strong Ties could be useful for getting at old varnish in difficult corners. These scrapers can be sharpened by running a fine file across the burr.

Varnish Touch-Up Bottle

Like many people who enjoy nicely varnished wood on their sailboats, Mike Collins, who sails his sloop, *Y-Knot,* out of Bloomington, Minnesota, dreaded getting out varnish, brushes, sandpaper, and brush cleaner every time he saw a little nick on a freshly finished surface. So he cleaned out a fingernail-polish bottle (which has a brush attached inside the cap) and attached a piece of sandpaper around the bottle with a rubber band. "Now when one of those uglies appears, I just break out my little bottle for an instant touch-up," says Collins. "This keeps out the moisture and helps prevent blistering."

Hand-Sanding Tool

Bob Whittier of Duxbury, Massachusetts, believes that there will always be a need for handsanding to give the delicate touch necessary in corners, grooves, and rounded spots. Hard-rubber sanding blocks aren't always appropriate because of their rigid structure. Abrasive paper wrapped around a standard blackboard eraser, available in any office-supply store, makes a versatile sanding tool. It will readily conform to many of the curved surfaces encountered in boat work, yet its rigid backbone makes it easy to hold and manipulate. Pressure is applied uniformly, and better work can be done with little risk of cutting through a fine finish.

Prop-Shaft Packing Removal

Anthony Pozsonyi of New York City has discovered a clever way to remove old flax packing from the stuffing box. He suggests straightening out an old fish hook of appropriate size, pushing the hook into the old flax packing and, with a slight twist of the straightened hook, locking the barb onto the fibers and pulling out the old packing.

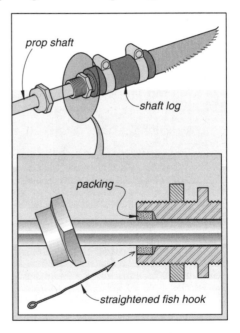

Autopilot Case

Bill Grabenstetter of Rochester, New York, has adapted a length of vinyl drain gutter to serve as a case for his tiller autopilot unit. He cut two pieces of gutter just longer than the autopilot unit and attached the two pieces with a long brass piano hinge. Teak trim strips down the length of the gutter pieces add lateral support to the box. Foam padding, cut to fit the autopilot and glued into the new box, keeps the unit snug. "Most autopilots are quite rugged, but this case provides enough extra protection that I now store my autopilot in a cockpit-seat locker instead of somewhere below out of reach," said Grabenstetter. The total cost was around $10.

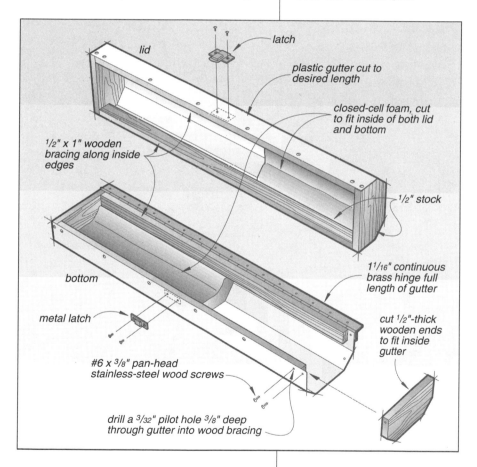

latch

lid

plastic gutter cut to desired length

closed-cell foam, cut to fit inside of both lid and bottom

$^1/_2$" x 1" wooden bracing along inside edges

$^1/_2$" stock

bottom

$1^1/_{16}$" continuous brass hinge full length of gutter

metal latch

cut $^1/_2$"-thick wooden ends to fit inside gutter

#6 x $^3/_8$" pan-head stainless-steel wood screws

drill a $^3/_{32}$" pilot hole $^3/_8$" deep through gutter into wood bracing

Rope-Work Tool

For marlinspike work R.F. Hunt of
Annapolis, Maryland, uses an electric
butane stove lighter to melt the ends of
synthetic lines, which prevents them from
fraying.

Heat the bitter end of the line until
soft. Work the hot end of the line against
a metal surface to form the end of the
line to any shape you want. It's easy to
make pointed ends on small-diameter
lines to form Turk's heads and the like, or
to make rounded ends on halyards and
sheets.

Portable Chart Table I

Richard Provost of Hartford, Connecticut, writes: "After several years of
sailing into unfamiliar harbors with a
chart stuffed under the cockpit cushion, I
decided to make a permanent arrangement. I took marine-grade plywood and
cut it to 24 inches by 18 inches, slightly
larger than the chart kit I use. I then
varnished it and attached a 22-inch by
17-inch piece of clear Lexan with two
hinges on the longer side. To hold the
Lexan securely over the chart, I used
plastic twist-style mirror holders, which I
found at the local hardware store. This
table is heavy enough to stay put on the
seat when I am sailing, so my chart is
readily visible. On boats with larger
cockpits, the table can be attached to the
aft end of the cabin house."

Portable Chart Table II

Chris Koina, who cruises and races on a 24-foot sloop in Mooloolaba, Queensland, Australia, has designed a surface, which is both inexpensive and lightweight, for plotting and storing charts on a boat without a built-in chart table.

with a curl at each end. The curl will hold up to six Admiralty charts or five U.S. Hydrographic Service charts. Chris tapes his charts into a roll to form a scroll, which he moves from one curl to the other to expose the portion he needs to reach the next point. This portable table stores inside his boat with simple clips attached to the cabintop. Turned upside down and placed across the cockpit, it serves as a cocktail table. You can

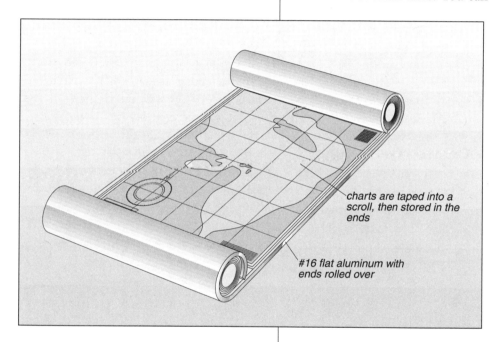

charts are taped into a scroll, then stored in the ends

#16 flat aluminum with ends rolled over

Chris had a sheet-metal shop roll the ends of a plate of 16-gauge aluminum to form a 17-inch-by-34-inch work surface

purchase a table in the size you need from Koina Manufacturing, P.O. Box 330, Moorooka, Queensland, Australia.

Portable Chart Table III

Kip Bodi of Laurel Hollow, New York, built a portable chart table for his Nonsuch 26, *Motivation*, that lies over the galley stove and even serves as additional counter space when not covered with charts.

The working surface of the chart table is ⅝-inch marine-grade plywood covered with a Formica-type laminate. He attached rubber bumpers to the base for skid resistance at the end of the table that rests on the galley counter. To the other edge of the table Bodi attached pieces of grooved oak flooring that fit snugly over the half-bulkhead rail. The dimensions, Bodi says, are not important because the concept must be adapted for different-size galleys. His, however, is designed to hold standard chart kits. To finish, he attached a carrying handle to the front of the table for easy offloading.

Simple Wire-Leading

M. Tompkins of Oklahoma City, Oklahoma, has a simple way to snake wires through tight confines.

To run small electrical wires through a narrow space between two surfaces (above the headliner, for instance), try using an old steel measuring tape. First, cut off the riveted tip of the tape (and the tape measure's pull tab), so you have a smooth piece of tape measure without any sharp edges or barbs. Then cut a small slice in the tape into which you can wedge a piece of string or fishing line. The string will act as the feeder line for rerunning the wire.

Next, carefully feed the tape from the rolled-up spool between the two surfaces. The rigid tape will turn corners with ease. Then tie the wire to the string and pull it through.

Jib Net

A jib net can keep sails or other gear from washing through your foredeck lifelines. Here's an idea from Skip Allan of Capitola, California, who fitted a simple and attractive one to his boat with minimal cost and labor. He used parachute cord and small padeyes. The padeyes were fixed to the deck at 12-inch centers, from the bow pulpit to the shrouds, as closely as possible to directly below the lifelines. The parachute cord was laced along from the bottom lifeline from the pulpit to the shrouds by alternately passing the line through the padeyes and over the lifeline. Skip then took another line, secured it at the pulpit, and laced it from the upper lifeline through the lower lacing and back to the upper lifeline. He tied off the end of the upper line with a rolling hitch to keep it from sliding.

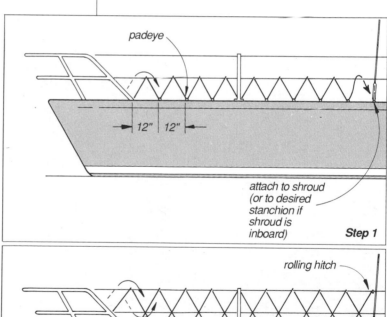

padeye

12" 12"

attach to shroud (or to desired stanchion if shroud is inboard)

Step 1

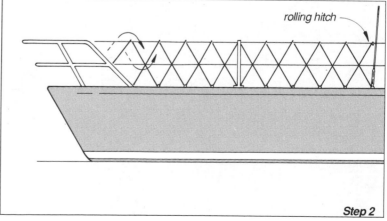

rolling hitch

Step 2

Under-the-Seat Stowage

Easy-to-reach, quick-access storage for bulky items you use on deck is difficult to find. Jack Niday, who sails an Ericson 35 out of Balboa Island, California, has attached two pieces of ¾-inch dowel stock lengthwise under his helmsman's seat as an excellent storage rack for his dock lines. Because the seat is curved and the space inside it is deep, it can accommodate all the necessary lines and keep them tangle free.

On *Puffin*, Doug Schmuck's 28-foot Bristol Channel cutter, which is currently sailing the South Pacific, the hatch in the helmsman's seat is flat and offers only 2 inches or so of storage space. But he found an excellent use for the space. Emergency cable cutters are held against the underside of the hatch by secure quick-release holders, making them readily available.

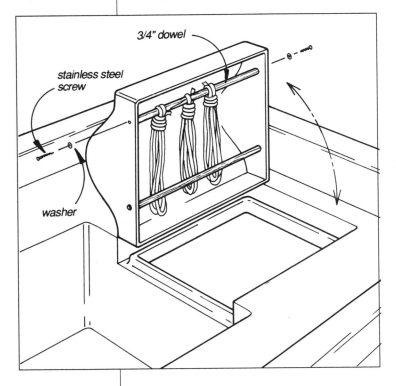

stainless steel screw

3/4" dowel

washer

Efficient Ground-Tackle Storage

As is true on many production boats, the forepeak area divided off for ground tackle in L.J. Ellis's Bristol 32 sloop *Chelsea* is far larger than necessary. Ellis created an

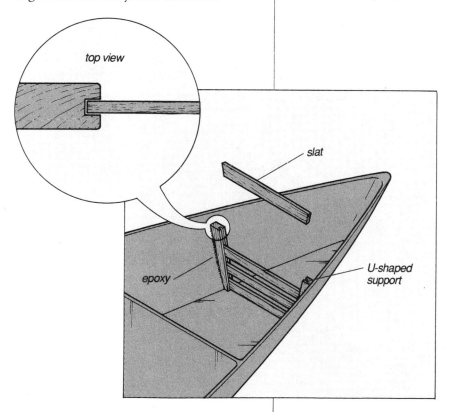

top view

slat

epoxy

U-shaped support

be easily removed for a cleanout.

An idea that could be incorporated into this forepeak divider to make the space forward of the slat-type bulkhead even more useful comes from Mike Goldenberg of Roslyn Heights, New York. Mike solved the problem of carrying two anchor rodes in the forepeak of his Bristol 40 ketch and at the same time keeping them clear of each

excellent place to carry spare sails and overnight bags by mounting two U-shaped pieces of pine, held in place against the hull with marine epoxy, halfway forward in the compartment. Removable slats fit into the U grooves; they are cut so they leave gaps for ventilation and drainage. The slats can

other. He divided the locker along the centerline using a ¾-inch-thick piece of plywood cut to shape and taped and epoxied in place. This divider can be fitted along the centerline, as drainage would be provided by the athwartships slats recommended by Ellis.

Hatchboard Holder

Finding a place to put the hatchboards is one of sailing's greatest puzzles. Sandra Kelting Prendergast aboard *Ka Sandera* has an answer for boats with a two-board companionway that could be adapted for most boats with opening hatchboards.

She leaves the bottom hatchboard in place, as it is easy to step over and provides addi-tional protection for belowdecks. Aft of this board, on the cockpit side of the companionway, she attached two small grooved strips identical to the track into which the hatchboards normally slide. The strips are through-bolted to the cabinhouse and hold the upper hatchboard securely against the lower hatchboard. Be sure to allow enough room for the hatchboards to swell when wet.

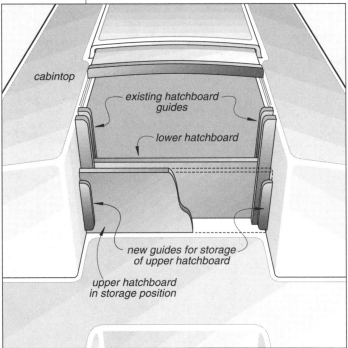

cabintop

existing hatchboard guides

lower hatchboard

new guides for storage of upper hatchboard

upper hatchboard in storage position

Propane Abroad

After sailing most of the way around the world aboard *Tine*, Penelope O. Brown was surprised to find that it was hard to get her U.S. propane bottles filled in Europe. Her "fill your own bottle" solution takes advantage of the liquid state of the fuel.

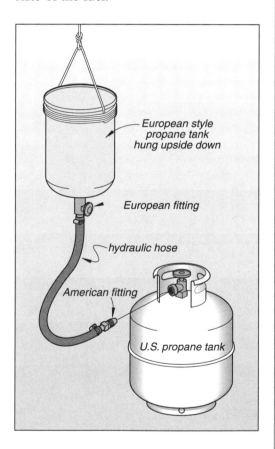

European style propane tank hung upside down

European fitting

hydraulic hose

American fitting

U.S. propane tank

With a European fitting, an American (or British) fitting, and a 3-foot length of hydraulic hose, you can make up an easily stowed connection that allows you to buy the local gas in their bottle, fill your own bottle, and return the local bottle. The reason for hydraulic hose is that the gas is under pressure and may burst low-pressure hose.

Since the propane is in a liquid state, the law of gravity prevails. There is pressure in both tanks so the flow will be slow. Keep the bottle to be filled below the lowest point of the bottle doing the filling. Check your progress by weighing the bottle with a fish scale from time to time. On a hot day you can speed up the process by putting the empty bottle on ice, or pouring cold water on it. As with any flammable product, care in handling is a must. Transfer the propane while ashore.

Boathook Storage

Paul Smith aboard *Spindrift*, a sailing salmon trawler whose home port is Bodega Bay, California, finds that the backstay or a shroud is the right place to store the boathook and has come up with a simple and functional way to keep it there. He purchased a small PVC pipe-reduction fitting that is large enough to fit the head of the boathook into. Then he lashed the fitting to the backstay with heavy twine a few feet above the transom. At the other end of the boathook, he drilled a small hole in the handle and looped a piece of line through it. To secure the boathook on the backstay, Smith sets the head of the hook in the pipe fitting and loops the other end around the backstay.

Cooking-Alcohol Container

Emma Smith of Granby, Connecticut, has found an easy way to pour stove alcohol into one of the canisters on her Origo stove. She uses a small shampoo bottle, the type found in professional hair salons, with a nozzle that can be turned

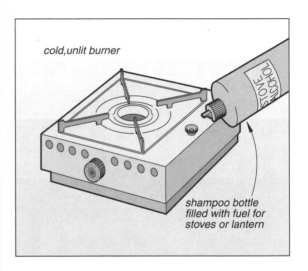

cold, unlit burner

shampoo bottle filled with fuel for stoves or lantern

up when you are ready to use it or down for storage. The nozzle makes it easy to pour the alcohol directly into the wick of the canister. The container is small, easier to store, and handy to reach. Place masking tape on the bottle and use a permanent marker to label the bottle as a non–hair-care product. **(Do not try to fill a lit stove.)**

Roto-Rooter Replaced

Arty Wener of Jericho, New York, has an interesting method for clearing stopped hoses, lines, drains, and clogged through-hull-piping, etc., that can't be snaked out due to 90-degree turns. He has discovered that a manual (or electric) air pump for inflating dinghies comes with tapered plastic fittings of various sizes. By inserting one of these fittings into the hose and pumping air into the line, most stoppages can be cleared out. It is also possible with some pumps to do the reverse and suck the stoppage through.

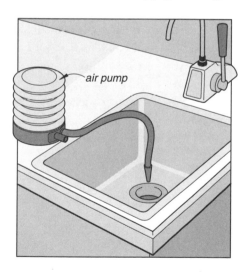

air pump

Combination Pump

Galley sink awash? John Hollands, currently cruising Fijian waters, has a solution that serves two purposes: using a manual pump and two-way valve to drain either your sink or bilge. He recommends connecting "a high-capacity manual bilge pump to the outlet side of a two-way selector valve, with the outlet side of the pump plumbed to the sink's through-hull seacock via a non-collapsible 1½-inch hose. The two inlet ports of the valve are then connected to the sink drain and the bilge. By selecting one or the other, you can use the pump to empty the sink and drain hose, eliminating the saltwater and odor problem; or you can use the same pump and through-hull to empty the bilge. You'll have to find room for the system under the sink. An access door to the sink drain and pump handle is a prerequisite. The fact that the sink drain must be kept closed after pumping to prevent salt water from backing up into the sink provides an extra measure of safety."

Instant Cockpit Cover and More

Lin and Larry Pardey carry two multi-purpose canvas cloths, one 4 feet by 6 feet and the other 4 feet by 4 feet, on board *Taleisin*. You can make them from a heavy, white synthetic canvas such as Acrylon, which is not only easy to sew but is less likely to flap in the wind. The cloth should have a 2-inch-wide tabling around all four edges. Corner grommets (either spur tooth or sewn rings) should be firmly secured with extra stitching or webbing to spread the strains. Lengths of ³⁄₁₆-inch Dacron line should be spliced into each grommet.

The Pardeys use the larger one primarily as an at-sea cockpit cover. The best thing about it, besides its low cost, is that it can be rigged when it's needed and also quickly moved out of the way.

They use the smaller cloth as a simple windscoop when they lie at anchor. It works almost as well as more elaborate scoops and catches wind even if the boat veers 20 degrees to either side of head-to-wind. The lower line is secured below deck. They attach two lines to the upper corner, one led to the spinnaker-pole ring on the front of the mast, 7 feet above the deck, and the other to the forestay. They tie the port and starboard lines to the lifelines with clove hitches with a running bight, and can use them to adjust the scoop to compensate for any wind-against-tide angle the boat assumes. The scoop can be used in light wind. If a shower occurs, they untie the upper lines and drop the scoop down the forehatch.

These canvas squares have many other uses on board. For example, they can cover small on-deck paint or glue jobs in case of showers, act as cushion protectors during engine work, or be used as a collision mat to help stop water from flooding in if the hull is fractured.

Tiller Extension

J. William Arpin of St. Cloud, Florida, who singlehands his 17-foot catboat, found that his tiller was too short to allow him to move around the cockpit while keeping a hand on the helm. To lengthen the tiller and maintain the traditional look of his boat, he constructed a tiller extension from mahogany (other hardwoods could be used).

Purchase the piece of hardwood of your choice at a local chandlery. (If you have trouble finding the right type of wood, look in the Yellow Pages under "hardwoods" or "wood.") Buy a piece with the same dimensions as your tiller; its length should be 3½ times the distance you wish to extend the tiller.

From the new wood you will form two coupling pieces, the tiller extension, and two cross braces, which help secure

the coupling pieces to the original tiller. To make the cross braces, cut a piece 3 times the width of your tiller from the new length of wood. Cut this piece in half, lengthwise, to make a pair of cross braces. Cut the remaining piece into thirds.

Clamp the two coupling pieces to the tiller with C clamps, overlapping the end of the tiller by half the length of the coupling. Place the cross braces as shown, and pre-drill the braces and coupling pieces to prevent the wood from splitting when installing wood screws. Attach the couplings and the cross braces to the tiller using wood screws and epoxy.

After the epoxy has cured, slip the tiller extension between the couplings and secure it at the desired length with wood screws and epoxy. Let the epoxy cure, sand the assembly, and varnish it. Consider making a hand grip from lashing twine, a nice cosmetic detail. The result is a classic-looking addition to any boat.

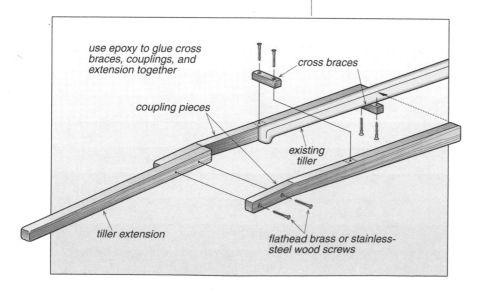

use epoxy to glue cross braces, couplings, and extension together

cross braces

coupling pieces

existing tiller

tiller extension

flathead brass or stainless-steel wood screws

Sailing Made Safer

*T*HERE'S A FABLE about a king's horse who lost a horseshoe nail . . . which caused the shoe to fall off . . . which caused the horse to go lame . . . which caused the king to lose the battle . . . and the kingdom. The old version of Murphy's Law. Unwilling to let onboard emergencies even start, the cruisers in this section of *SAIL's Things That Work* have created ingenious ways to make their boats safer.

Take George Reed, for instance, a former aeronautical engineer and company manager with 25 years of sailing experience aboard his boats in the Great Lakes and the Northeast. He retired to Edenton, North Carolina, with his new Nonsuch 30, which he and his wife cruise, and sometimes race, on Albemarle Sound.

While thinking about the safety equipment he would need for his new boat and concerned about his and his wife's ability to help get someone back aboard (they're in their late 60s), he invented the device described on page 38. It consists of a boat fender wrapped with polypropylene line, which, when thrown in the water, will spool out the line without tangles. If someone were to fall overboard, Reed says he would probably throw both his horseshoe ring and the Retriever, but he feels a conscious person has a pretty good chance of grabbing the floating polypropylene line and of guiding himself, or being pulled, to the boat's stern ladder.

Fortunately, Reed has never had to use his Retriever in a real emergency, but he, like all the cruisers in this section, thinks it's better to fight Murphy than join him.

Man-Overboard Float

George Reed of Edenton, North Carolina, dubbed his man-overboard recovery device the "Reed Retriever."

To make one of your own, tightly wrap a 50-foot length of polypropylene line around a round fender as shown in the figure. Tie the bitter end to a stern cleat or rail, and leave the float accessible. If someone goes over the side, drop the fender in the water. The tuck will pull out and the line will stream out behind the boat, free of tangles. The larger the float, the greater the device's buoyancy. Use polypropylene line because it floats.

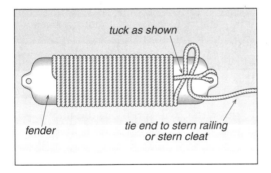

tuck as shown

fender

tie end to stern railing
or stern cleat

Singlehander's Last-Chance Lanyard

D.J. Young of Chorleywood, England, calls this safety line a "last-chance lanyard." He says, "Whenever I am sailing singlehanded I trail a line over the stern. It started as a trailed warp of about 15

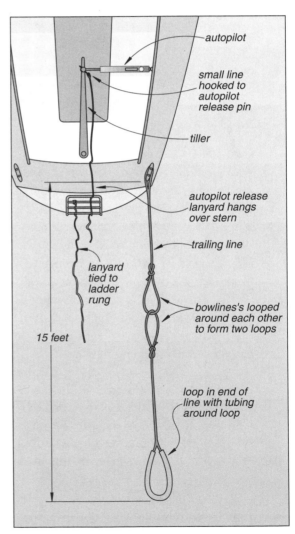

autopilot

small line
hooked to
autopilot
release pin

tiller

autopilot release
lanyard hangs
over stern

trailing line

lanyard
tied to
ladder
rung

bowlines's looped
around each other
to form two loops

15 feet

loop in end of
line with tubing
around loop

feet, but over the years I have added various improvements."

First he put a length of rubber tube over the end loop to keep the loop always open, making it easier to grab. Then he added a connector in the middle of the line to make it easier to haul oneself along it back to the boat. As an aside, he had never seen his method of making a connector in the middle of a line published before: It is made by tying two lengths of rope together using two bowlines, leaving a loop of any desired size between each of the knots. Young writes: "This has the advantage that the knots keep the connector spread open, whereas a spliced loop in the middle of a line closes up."

His boat has a stern boarding ladder that folds down from the stern pulpit, so he ties a lanyard to a rung so that the ladder falls into the down position if the lanyard is pulled. This means, of course, that the ladder must not be hooked into the stern pulpit while sailing. "I thought this arrangement could be dangerous if I were to fall against it. So I rigged up a short length of line across the gap in the stern pulpit and pulled it tight with a pelican hook. To keep the ladder in place I tied it to this short line with a breakable piece of twine."

Finally, he writes: "In order to disengage the autopilot (and hopefully have the boat round up into the wind and slow down) I hook a small line over the autopilot pin on the tiller so that, if the line is jerked, it will pull the push-pull arm off the pin."

Stronger Stanchions

By nature, stanchions and pulpits are susceptible to bending and distortion. If yours have suffered such abuse, or if you want to strengthen them beforehand to minimize bending, Skip Allan of Capitola, California, recommends inserting a dowel or broom handle into the stanchion tube as far as it will go. "The fit should be snug," he writes, "and persuasion can be applied with a rubber mallet. The added stiffness is substantial; you may even need to consider adding backing plates below decks."

Securing Lifelines

When Larry Marvel of Spokane, Washington, bought his San Juan 7.7, the one-piece single lifeline from the bow pulpit to the stern created problems. When he released the pelican hook to drop the lifeline for boarding, the entire lifeline dropped and the foredeck netting slackened. Not only was this unsafe, but the lifeline was also difficult to stretch back out again.

"I purchased two ¼-inch U-bolts and clamped each one on the lifeline immediately aft of the first stanchion forward of the boarding area on each side of the boat. I then took two 35mm film containers, with the lids attached, and drilled a ⁵⁄₁₆-inch hole through the top and the bottom. I split the canisters on one side down to the holes and slipped them over the U-bolts. Then I covered the canisters with white rigging tape. They are now the same color and diameter as my foam lifeline cover. When I release the lifeline only the cockpit section releases, and there is no more tangled netting on the bow."

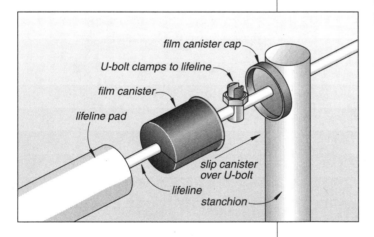

film canister cap

U-bolt clamps to lifeline

film canister

lifeline pad

slip canister over U-bolt

lifeline

stanchion

Dodger Guard

Canvas cockpit dodgers are vulnerable to falling booms and falling people; they also can make climbing into and out of the cockpit difficult, as they offer no firm handholds to hurrying crew. Allan Wallis, a New Zealand offshore sailor, solved both problems with a dodger guard.

The fabricated stainless-steel guard offers a firm hand grip and can also be used as a rack for solar panels. It is firmly

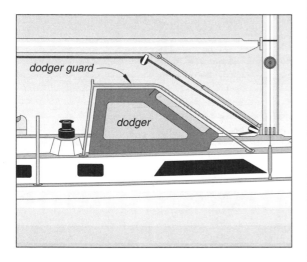

attached to the cabintop with backing plates beneath each of its four feet. A piece of wood could be bolted to the upper rail of the guard and notched to work as a boom gallows.

Boom Crutch

"We've never felt comfortable with the nearly universal practice of hanging the boom from the backstay when the mainsail is dropped and furled," write Natalie and Al Levy of Chicago, Illinois. "It would appear to put strain on the rigging, and it is often difficult for short sailors to reach up and clip the boom to the backstay. The swinging boom can make the crew furling the mainsail feel insecure. To make a boom crutch for our 22-foot Ensign, we purchased two ordinary broom handles and cut them down to fit the distance from the cockpit corner to a few inches above boom height. With the two broomsticks crossed to create an X, we drilled a hole and then inserted a bolt, using washers on both sides of the wood. We glued rubber cups meant for orthopedic crutches to the bottoms of the broomsticks to protect the cockpit surfaces. Spread open, the ends fit snugly into the cockpit corners, and the boom rests in the V. With the mainsheet cleated, the boom is secure, and the mainsail is easy to furl.

"You can scale up these sheerleg specs by checking out industrial-style push-broom handles in janitorial supply stores. Foam or felt padding can be glued to the V to protect both boom and crutch, though we have not found this padding necessary."

Intracoastal Waterway Anchor System

The sailor who plans a cruise along the ICW will often encounter muddy bottoms, limited swinging room, and, according to Phelps Tracy of Jamestown, Rhode Island, ample opportunity to run aground. Tracy and his wife, Becky, cruised for a year from the Bahamas to Rhode Island in their 30-foot Sea Sprite sloop. They found that the same gear used for anchoring had to be available for kedging.

Tracy writes: "Basically, my gear is a double-ended anchor rode with a 25-pound CQR anchor at one end, with 8 feet of ⅜-inch chain leading to an extra 8 feet of ½-inch chain; and then 160 feet of anchor rode shackled to 12 feet of ⅜-inch chain and a 12-pound high-tensile Danforth at the far end. The CQR rests on the bow roller, while the rest of the gear resides in a plastic milk crate, Danforth anchor at the bottom. We lash the crate on deck near the shrouds. It would not be a good idea in really rough seas, but it is handy going down the ICW.

"Between Rhode Island and Cape May we used the plow exclusively. The addition of the ½-inch chain added the weight we needed to help the anchor work. We also found the larger-diameter chain picked up less mud than smaller sizes.

"Once we reached Cape May, we almost never anchored in more than 15 feet of water and, because of currents and sometimes crowded anchorages, we had to limit our swing. With everything ready on deck, it was easy to put out two anchors and secure to the middle of the rode, Bahamian style.

"Like many people who transit the ICW, we ran aground quite often. The CQR proved too heavy and awkward to use as a kedge. The 12-pound Danforth on its 12 feet of chain was easier to work with. Although we always ran aground going forward, we found the best arrangement for getting unstuck was to row out the kedge with the rode running through the bow chock and then aft to our primary winch. Becky would tail and I would crank until the bow was headed out toward deeper water (pulling from the stern never worked well). We then had the bow pointing in the right direction and, with the power of the motor, came off easily."

Having found the ICW as grounding-prone as the Tracys did, Lin and Larry Pardey note the convenience of their system for fast kedging. It is far easier to load a milk crate of tackle into the stern of the dinghy and then row away from the boat, letting the line play out until the anchor is clear to let go, than it is to dig out the gear and pile it into the dinghy when things are already a little confused by the grounding. One additional thought: It takes less effort to play out the line as you row than to try to drag a kedge line through the water to get it taut.

Remote Tiller Steering

Al O'Neill of Newark, Delaware, has jury-rigged a device for remote steering when weighing anchor singlehanded.

A common technique for breaking the anchor free when it's firmly set is to motor forward, taking up slack as you go. When the rode is straight up and down, you take a turn around a cleat so that the

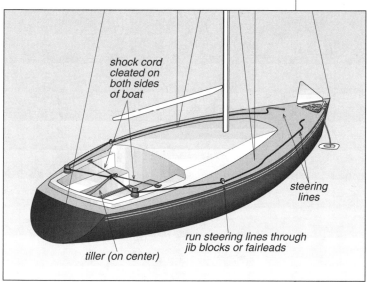

shock cord cleated on both sides of boat

tiller (on center)

run steering lines through jib blocks or fairleads

steering lines

boat's inertia plus engine power break the anchor loose. Only then is muscle power required, as you raise the anchor from the bottom to the deck and stow it. Very

simple, except when one is singlehanding in a crowded anchorage. "Spending that much time up forward, away from the helm, with the boat under way, can be a scary experience—for you and your neighbor," says O'Neill.

For his tiller-steered boat, O'Neill has developed a simple way to remove a fair amount of the unwanted suspense in getting away from an anchorage. To set up the rig, he centerlines his tiller and then leads equal lengths of shock cord from the tiller to cleats on either side of the cockpit coaming. There should be enough tension in the shock cords to keep the tiller centerlined when released.

Next, he ties two longer pieces of nonelastic line to the tiller, and runs them around the jib blocks (or through fairleads) on either side of the boat, and forward to the bow. The resulting configuration allows him to stand on the bow and, by pulling on the two lines, to use the tiller.

With the engine engaged or a significant way on, this method can present a degree of risk, unless the steering lines are led far enough aft to allow the tiller's full range of steering.

Easy Spinnaker Handling

Julie Palm, aboard the Tayana 52 *Sojourner,* offers a solution for shorthanded spinnaker handling. She finds that a spinnaker trip line allows the crew to take down the chute with as few as two people— one in the cockpit and one on the foredeck. As a result, flying the spinnaker has become *Sojourner's* normal downwind sailplan.

"We use a light ¼-inch trip line about 15 feet long. When setting up our spinnaker pole, the foredeck person threads the trip line forward through the downhaul shackle on the bottom of the pole, through the release ring of the guy shackle, and back through a padeye on top of the pole. A figure eight or other stopper knot is tied at the forward end of the line. The other end is tied to a lifeline with enough slack so the pole can move freely without tripping the guy.

"When it is time to lower the chute, the foredeck person pulls the trip line to release the guy and then pulls the take-down line for the spinnaker sock. No one has to stand precariously on the bow pulpit to 'stab' the guy shackle. We now feel safe and secure, knowing we can always release the guy from the chute quickly in a sudden gust."

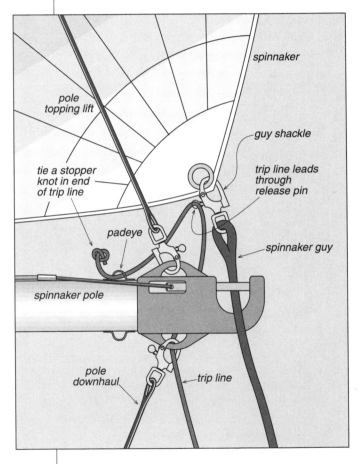

spinnaker

pole topping lift

guy shackle

tie a stopper knot in end of trip line

trip line leads through release pin

padeye

spinnaker guy

spinnaker pole

pole downhaul

trip line

44

Outboard Hoist

David Comerzan, aboard the ketch *Misty*, has found that lifting an 84-pound outboard 5 feet up onto the deck can be quite a challenge.

"I quickly saw the advantage of using the mizzenboom with a block-and-tackle as a kind of crane," he says. "Rather than trust my ability to tie a sturdy knot, I stitched a sling of 1-inch nylon webbing to snugly fit the head of the outboard. I attached an eyebolt at the end of the boom to which I hook the block-and-tackle. Once attached to the outboard, the system easily pulls the outboard up and over the deck."

For sloops and cutters, the mainboom and a preventer can also be used. In all cases, be sure the topping lift is extra sturdy to support the weight of the outboard.

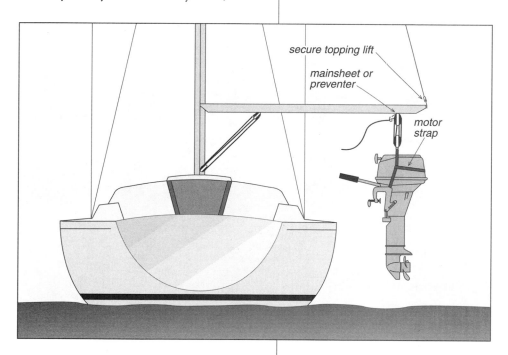

secure topping lift

mainsheet or preventer

motor strap

Topping-Lift Control

Michael Koppstein of Ogunquit, Maine, developed an innovative mainboom topping-lift control. Traditionally, the topping lift is either left to flog around while the mainsail is hoisted, or it is connected to a long length of shock cord run from the deck up the backstay to a swivel, whipped onto the backstay, and then redirected and attached via a thimble to the topping lift. This system requires adjustment according to point of sail and has limited life and looks.

Koppstein's innovation involves two small blocks, one with a sheave that fits the topping-lift wire and one that fits the backstay wire. To set up your own control, start by disassembling each block and reassembling each one around the cable that it fits.

While your vessel is tied up at a dock, lift the boom to the height it achieves with the mainsail raised. Send a crewmember up the backstay in a bosun's chair to approximately the height of the first spreader (or halfway up the mainsail luff). Tighten the topping lift and measure the distance between it and the backstay. Cut a piece of shock cord 6 inches shorter than this distance and whip each end to one of the blocks.

Now the blocks will run up and down the backstay with changes in the tension on the shock cord. The "bungy block" system keeps the topping lift from chafing and disturbing wind release on the mainsail leech.

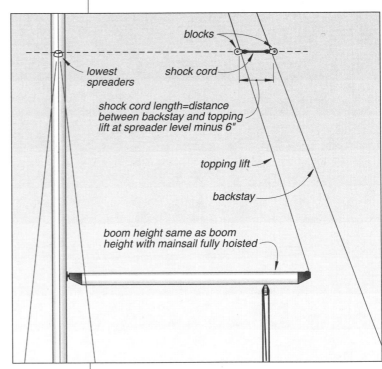

blocks

lowest spreaders

shock cord

shock cord length=distance between backstay and topping lift at spreader level minus 6"

topping lift

backstay

boom height same as boom height with mainsail fully hoisted

Topping-Lift Ring

Conrad and Charlotte Skladal of Sunny-vale, California, have been cruising on *Wisp* for more than 10 years. One modification they made as they sailed provides extra places to secure lines at deck level without using cleats. They

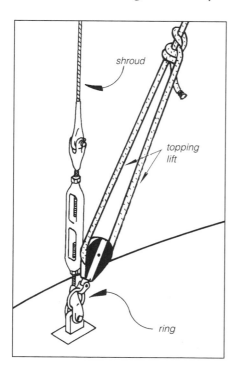

write: "We have found 2-inch-diameter stainless-steel rings (made of ⅛-inch tubing) to be very useful as an attachment point for the ends of halyards, as well as for keeping the main topping lift secure. We simply slipped the rings between our turnbuckle toggle and the turnbuckle on the lower shrouds.

"To make an adjustable topping lift, we shackled a single block to the ring and led the bitter end of the topping lift through the block and up to where we secured it back on itself with a rolling hitch. We can adjust the height of the end of the mainboom by sliding the rolling hitch up and down the standing line. There's no need for a cleat, and the deck is clear of lines."

Through-the-Deck Fittings

When installing stanchions and other through-the-deck fittings, careful attention must be given to sealing the fastenings. According to Larry Gonzalez of Plantation, Florida, threads tend to wipe off sealer as they are pressed into a hole. Because of this "wiping" action, leaks occur. To prevent water from seeping down through such fittings, countersink the hole in the deck in order for the sealer (when hardened) to act as an O-ring.

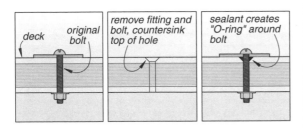

deck — original bolt

remove fitting and bolt, countersink top of hole

sealant creates "O-ring" around bolt

Testing for Rigging Flaws

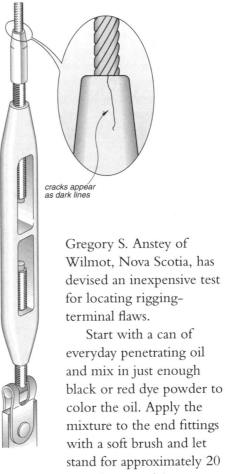

cracks appear as dark lines

Gregory S. Anstey of Wilmot, Nova Scotia, has devised an inexpensive test for locating rigging-terminal flaws.

Start with a can of everyday penetrating oil and mix in just enough black or red dye powder to color the oil. Apply the mixture to the end fittings with a soft brush and let stand for approximately 20 minutes. Use a rag dampened (not soaked) with a solvent such as alcohol to remove the excess oil/dye mixture from the fitting. Then apply a light coat of talc or baby powder to the fitting and let it stand approximately 10 minutes. Now you are ready to inspect the fittings; a crack will appear as a red or black (depending on the dye used) line on the powder.

Fixing a Leaky Rudderpost

Charles H. Cook Jr. of New Wilmington, Pennsylvania, has found a do-it-yourself solution for an inboard rudderpost leak aboard his tiller-steered boat. As a waterproof sleeve he used a piece of semiflexible ABS plastic tubing with an inside diameter just larger than the outside diameter of the rudderpost. He cut the sleeve to a length that reaches from the inside of the hull to the underside of the cockpit sole. Then he split the sleeve lengthwise to allow it to be fitted over the rudderpost.

The split can be sealed with fiberglass tape, epoxy resin, and/or epoxy putty after the sleeve is fitted into place. The ends of this sleeve are sealed to the bottom of the cockpit sole and the inside bottom of the hull with the same materials. WEST System compounds work well. A few wraps of tape will hold the split closed while the seal sets. Once installed, this sleeve harmlessly confines any water that squeezes through the rudderpost bearing.

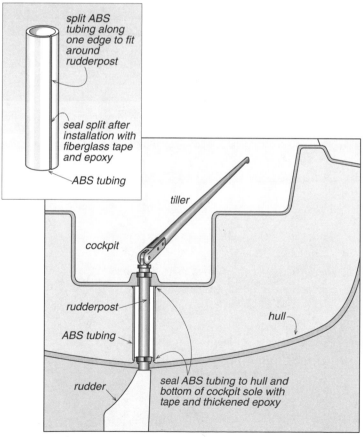

split ABS tubing along one edge to fit around rudderpost

seal split after installation with fiberglass tape and epoxy

ABS tubing

tiller

cockpit

rudderpost

ABS tubing

hull

rudder

seal ABS tubing to hull and bottom of cockpit sole with tape and thickened epoxy

49

Avoid Through-Hull Drilling

Bruce Fallert of Fort Myers, Florida, found an easy way to internally mount a depthsounder transducer to the hull of his 26-foot Marie/Holm Folkboat, *Spirit Level*, without through-hull drilling. He took a plumber's PVC pipe-reducer fitting and shaped it to fit the inside curve of the boat's hull. Then he glued the pipe fitting to the inside of the hull with a silicone sealant to form a water-tight seal. Next he drilled a small hole in the shoulder of the fitting so he could later fill the gap between hull and transducer with water. Finally, he glued the transducer to the pipe fitting and filled the fitting with water. The water keeps an airtight, liquid contact between the inside of the hull and the transducer, allowing the unit to function without drilling a hole in the hull.

To shape the PVC pipe fitting, Fallert used a cabinetmaker's curve, an angle finder, and a level (to ensure upright mounting of the transducer). He dyed the water with a few drops of food coloring to monitor for leaks. After filling, he covered the drilled hole with a rubber plug so he could top off the water if evaporation occurred. (He hasn't needed to refill in two years.)

Two factors need to be considered. Be sure to place the pipe fitting over solid laminating, not cored portions of the hull. A transducer won't read through air

in the core construction. Also, water could present a problem in freezing temperatures and should be drained if there is a chance of freezing.

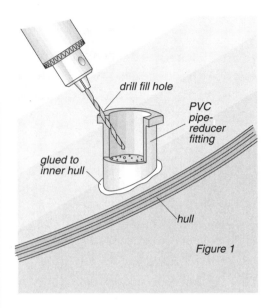

drill fill hole

PVC pipe-reducer fitting

glued to inner hull

hull

Figure 1

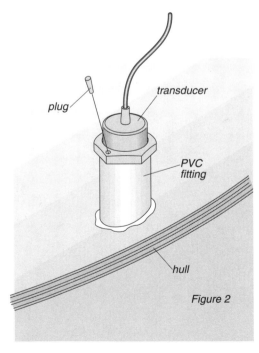

plug

transducer

PVC fitting

hull

Figure 2

Eyebolts Instead of Padeyes

Any time you can make one piece of gear serve two purposes afloat, you come out a winner. Charles Rice of Goldsboro, North Carolina, needed a strong point to which he could secure a safety-harness tether just outside the companionway of his pocket cruiser. He considered through-bolting a padeye at each side of the companionway. At the same time, he realized he needed a strong point inside the cabin to which he could secure the large icechest that also serves as the cabin step and occasional seat.

To save the cost and installation time, he combined the two necessities. He installed stainless-steel eyebolts with eye nuts through the cabin back, using a large-diameter washer for backing on each side of the bulkhead. Instead of having to drill three holes each for two separate sets of padeyes, he had one hole to drill and one eye nut to thread into place for an inside/outside attachment of exceptional strength.

Rings Instead of Pins

Nick Reynolds of Vancouver, Washington, uses clevis rings instead of cotter pins on his boat's turnbuckles. Reynolds writes: "These are the little stainless wire rings that hold clevis pins in place. Installation takes two twisting efforts for each clevis ring. First I twist the ring on the body of the turnbuckle (open-bodied turnbuckles only, of course), and then I repeat the process to get the ring in the hole in the end of the threaded portion of the turnbuckle. When I remove the ring for adjustment, I can't lose it because it is still around the body of the turnbuckle. The change meets all my objectives: It holds the turnbuckle; it doesn't tear the sail; it looks good; and it's really cheap—less than $3 for the 25-footer I sail."

Taming the Gimballed Stove

Cruiser Tom Linskey writes: "On our 28-foot fiberglass-hulled Bristol Channel cutter *Freelance*, Harriet and I found our gimballed stove to be a mixed blessing. It's great to have a level cooking surface when the boat is heeled or rolling, but in

bolted a brass barrel bolt (the kind with a nylon friction pad that keeps the bolt in position) onto the lower lip of the stove. I scribed the arc the stove makes when swinging onto a piece of ⅛-inch brass plate and mounted that onto a teak riser that brought the plate up next to the barrel bolt. Then I drilled and filed out latch holes in the plate for various angles of heel and on the level.

"While most times at sea we just let the stove do its own gimballing thing, in rough seas we can now lock it to approximate our angle of heel and use deep pots and pot holders if we feel that that is safer. In quiet ports

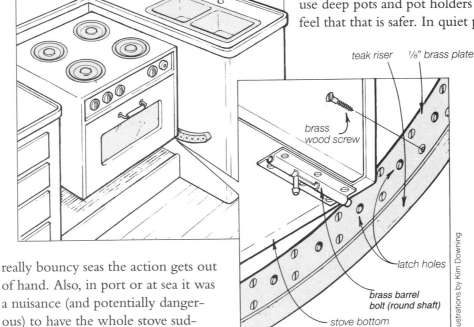

teak riser   ⅛" brass plate

brass wood screw

latch holes

brass barrel bolt (round shaft)

stove bottom

Illustrations by Kim Downing

really bouncy seas the action gets out of hand. Also, in port or at sea it was a nuisance (and potentially dangerous) to have the whole stove suddenly pivot when the oven door was opened. Ideally, we wanted to be able to choose between a freely gimballing stove and one that could be locked on the level or at any angle of heel when we needed a non-swinging surface.

"To tame our gimballed stove, I

we usually just secure it on the level, and, if the top burners are heavily freighted with boiling pots, we lock it before opening the oven door."

Portlight Covers

Alexander Yaxis of Amityville, New York, wrote regarding his concerns about using cloth curtains on teak rods aboard his H–28 ketch: "They are a fire hazard if they are near the galley, harbor mildew, fade, require careful washing, block out sunlight, and are not neat or shipshape." His solution: portlight-shaped translucent ovals of 1/16-inch-thick semiflexible translu-

cent plastic (Poly-plastics's Pan-lon) plus two roundhead screws.

He cut the plastic 1/2 inch larger than the portlight, then notched each end as shown in the figure. Two roundhead wood screws are positioned at each end of the portlight to hold the solid "curtains." To put the curtains up, he bends the plastic into a curve; it snaps into place. When not in use, the curtains are stowed flat under a bunk cushion. These curtains will work equally well for opening ports as long as the screws are positioned on the opening flange.

For boats with bronze or alloy portlight frames, sheet-metal screws or roundhead machine screws can be used instead of wood screws. Another useful adaptation would be to carry a set of opaque or very dark-colored "curtains" to darken the interior of the boat and help the early-morning off-watch to get a sounder sleep.

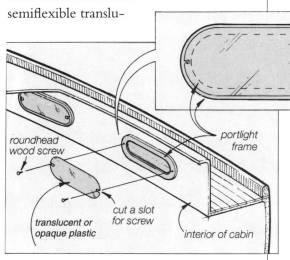

roundhead
wood screw

portlight
frame

cut a slot
for screw

translucent or
opaque plastic

interior of cabin

Dinghy Oar Rack

Pat and Paul Janson, who cruise the Chesapeake on their Bristol 29.9, *Ardea*, deflate their small inflatable dinghy when they are not using it and stow it in its bag. Paul found packing the oars and wooden seat in the same bag made storing the dinghy in a cockpit locker difficult. He also worried that sharp edges and corners of the collapsible oars would cause wear and tear on both the dinghy and the bag. So he devised the two-part rack shown in the figure and doubled the usefulness of his

hanging locker by screwing the rack inside against a bulkhead. A shock cord restraint keeps the oars from rattling. The seat slips into the corner behind the oar rack. Angling the cutouts for the blades makes the rack as compact as possible. The total cost is minimal, and only simple tools are needed.

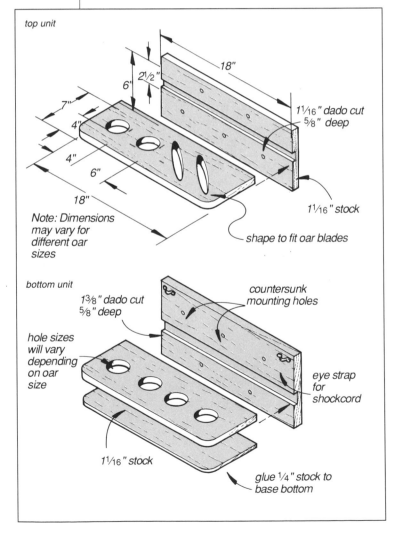

top unit

18"

2½"

6"

7"

4"

4"

6"

18"

1¹⁄₁₆" dado cut
⅝" deep

1¹⁄₁₆" stock

shape to fit oar blades

Note: Dimensions may vary for different oar sizes

bottom unit

1³⁄₈" dado cut
⅝" deep

countersunk mounting holes

hole sizes will vary depending on oar size

eye strap for shockcord

1¹⁄₁₆" stock

glue ¼" stock to base bottom

Propane Storage

Kathy Bahen, aboard *Highbanks,* has devised a propane tank housing for above-deck use.

She writes, "Since space was limited on our 35-foot Allied Seabreeze cruising sloop, we did not want to convert valuable locker space for propane storage." They also did not want two exposed tanks on deck subjected to the weather.

To alleviate this problem, Kathy suggests the following steps:

1. Purchase one long section of PVC sewer pipe, with enough diameter to fit the tanks but not with too much movement.

2. Cut lengths to allow for the height of the tank plus lid, the regulator, and a ½-inch wood base for the tanks. Cut a circular piece of plywood as the interior base and fasten or epoxy it in place. (The wood base helps prevent any rust on deck or scarring from tanks.)

3. Measure the outside diameter of the PVC pipe and cut the lid to match.

4. Cut two strips of 1-inch stock to match the inside diameter of the PVC; epoxy and screw onto the center of the underside of each wooden lid. Be sure to allow space at each end so

the strip will fit inside the pipe and the lid will sit flush on top.

5. Place the lids on the PVC pipe. Be sure to mark where the ends hit inside. Drill one hole on each side of the PVC pipe through to the base support. This allows you to pin the lids on. Attach with cotter pins on a line that is tied to the backstay; then you will always know where the pins are.

6. At the base of one pipe, cut a notch for the hose; then run the propane line through the lazarette to the stove.

7. Place both tanks on the transom and secure them with battery straps to the backstay or stern pulpit.

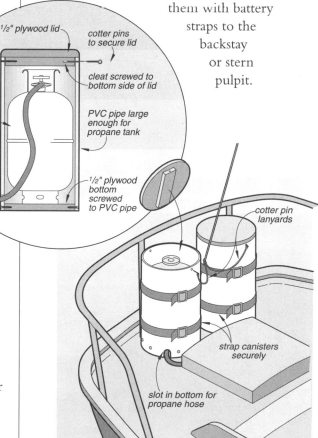

½" plywood lid

cotter pins to secure lid

cleat screwed to bottom side of lid

PVC pipe large enough for propane tank

propane tank

½" plywood bottom screwed to PVC pipe

cotter pin lanyards

strap canisters securely

slot in bottom for propane hose

Instrument-Panel Protection

Richard Coerse of Alexandria, Virginia, decided to make the instrument panel on his boat less prone to the damage that can be caused by a wayward winch handle, deck shoe, or the sun. For less than $6, he added a Lexan panel cover, using the same screws to mount both the panel and the cover. He then cut out just enough of the Lexan to allow access to the key and starter switch.

He stitched a sun cover of acrylic sail-cover fabric, and sandwiched the fabric between the top edges of the Lexan and the panel-mounting flange. He added a couple of snap fasteners below the panel so the acrylic can be rolled down over the Lexan and snapped in place. He rolls up the fabric when he needs to see the

instruments. Shaded by the acrylic, his instruments will keep looking new and unfaded for years, and it is unlikely that the glass faces of the oil-pressure and temperature gauges will crack.

The Pardeys add the following note: With this or any other on-deck key installation, it is imperative that your key switch be waterproof; otherwise, a damp-induced short could burn out your starter motor. Do not assume your switch is waterproof until you check it.

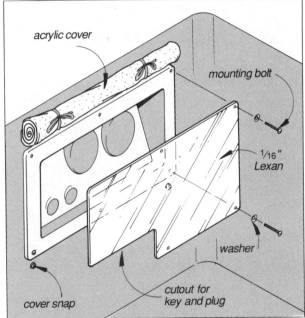

acrylic cover

mounting bolt

1/16" Lexan

washer

cover snap

cutout for key and plug

Waterproof Instrument-Back Covers

When John Snyder took delivery of his new 30-foot sloop in Deerfield Beach, Florida, he was distressed to find the dealer had installed the log and depthsounder on the cockpit bulkhead with the instrument backs protruding into the head. There they were, delicate electronic devices, some with the connecting wires exposed, just waiting for the first hot shower to accelerate normal shipboard corrosion.

Snyder first tried to purchase watertight covers. Then, as he writes, the perfect solution turned up on the supermarket shelf: "Plastic food containers. If I fastened the lid to the bulkhead, I could remove the bowl to service the instruments. I bought a Rubbermaid Servin-Saver 1.2 quart container for $1.25 and cut a hole in the lid large enough to go over the instrument back. I then screwed each lid fast to the bulkhead after laying a bead of sealant around the hole. I used four stainless-steel screws per lid and was careful to position them so the screw heads would not be under the instrument bracket when I reinstalled it. Then I reattached the instruments.

"Now I simply snap the bowl of the food container into the airtight seal of the lid, and the instruments are air- and watertight, and covered by an easily removable translucent cover. For further protection you could put a small envelope of silica gel inside each bowl to combat moisture.

Vent Restrainers

Snap-in plastic cowl vents can easily fly overboard if they are kicked loose. Emil Gaynor of Camarillo, California, sent in this idea, one he uses on his Cal 2-46. The restraining chain and bar are simple to install. They keep the vent from going overboard but allow it to be removed easily or rotated when necessary.

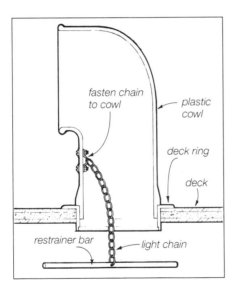

fasten chain to cowl

plastic cowl

deck ring

deck

restrainer bar

light chain

Protect Your Pump

Michael Beerli of Sarasota, Florida, has a solution for the irritating problem of a pressurized water system that continues to run after the tank is empty. Very often the sound of the pump cannot be heard over engine noise or by those on deck, and many pumps are damaged by prolonged running without water.

A small indicator light can be installed in the pump circuit so that any time the system is activated, the light illuminates. A 12-volt DC red, blue, or green pilot light, available at electronic and automotive stores, works nicely. Simply wire the light in parallel to and between the pressure switch and the pump motor.

Protection for Electrical Connections

Charles C. Squires of Kilmaranock, Virginia, tells us that he hears a lot of complaints about electronic equipment on boats. "Failure is usually caused by corroded connections. I think I have solved a big part of these troubles on my boat.

"Start by cleaning the connection until it is shiny. Make a good, tight joint, and then paint the area with fingernail polish. *Voilà!* You have a color-coded, watertight seal that will last a long time."

Dimples That Can Save Your Blocks

Charles Rice of Goldsboro, North Carolina, remembered the skinned knees he got as a youngster when the nuts vibrated loose from his roller skates and the wheels fell off. He solved that problem by putting the point of a steel punch into the thread seam between the nut and the axle and giving it a sharp blow with a hammer, which left a dimple in the metal that locked the nut in place. Now that he sails and no longer skates, the same dimples have found their way onto his boat.

To keep deck hardware from being easily removed when his boat is unattended, he puts three large dimples, 120 degrees apart, at the threaded end of the shackles holding his jibsheet-lead blocks. To remove the screw from the shackle now requires two large wrenches. The same dimples will act as locks to keep any nut, such as engine-mounting nuts and the nuts bolting your spreaders to the mast, from backing off because of vibration; adding security will cost nothing but a sharp tap with a hammer and a steel punch.

"Green" Epoxy Cleaner

Peter Martyn of Toronto, Ontario, uses a lot of epoxy to keep his traditional wooden cutter, *Hispaniola*, seaworthy. Sticky fingers have been a problem. After much testing he's found an environmentally friendly cleaner that reduces the need for "reeking, skin-drying, flammable, expensive, and fast-evaporating" acetone. The miracle compound is white vinegar.

Soak a clean rag in vinegar to scrub uncured epoxy resin off fingers, tools, and resin tins. Vinegar is kinder than acetone to your skin, your nose, and the environment. If you need more cleaning power for partly cured resin, mix only a small amount of acetone with the vinegar.

Protect Your Fingers

Lin Pardey writes: "As a mad varnisher, I had come to dread the damage sanding did to my fingertips. I tried using masking tape to keep from wearing through my skin. It worked, but got messy if the tape got wet, left goo behind when I pulled the protectors off, and wore out quite quickly. Then I found a product designed for production workers in the electronic assembly business and for jewelers who must handle a lot of abrasives in their work.

"Guard Tex safety tape, made by General Bandages, Inc. (P.O. Box 909, Morton Grove, Illinois 60053), is rubber (latex)-coated gauze that sticks to itself. It is easy to wrap around your fingers and readily tears into appropriate lengths. It helps you grip tools and sandpaper better and works well when wet. For wet-sanding the bottom of a race boat, for rubbing down varnish work, for any job with abrasives, this tape is well worth the price of just over $1 a roll. Three-quarter-inch-wide tape comes in packages of 16; each roll is 30 yards long."

Sailing Made More Fun

Remember when you were a little kid—those kick-back, giggly, hazy-crazy days on the water? Maybe you just had a leaky pram with one oar or, if you were really lucky, a dinghy that sailed. No matter. The water fights and bumper-boats were great, and when the wind was right, you felt you could sail the world. Now modern Peter Pans are finding all kinds of ways to make their grownup boats just as much fun . . . ways to stow more toys, such as sailboards, ways to turn the cockpit into a heck of a party platform.

After a cruise with friends on Lake Erie, which aerospace engineer Robert Miner describes as "the nicest week in the last century," he was hooked, buying first an S2 9.2, then a few years later a Tanzer 29, and finally a Gozzard 31. He and his wife wanted to enjoy sunset meals in the cockpit of the Tanzer; but with a tiller, the boat had no pedestal to which a table could be attached. "I thought about it for a couple of years, then built it over one winter," said Miner, who came up with the simple-to-build and eminently workable plan described in this section of *SAIL's Things That Work*. Thus inspired, he worked with Ted Gozzard, the builder of his latest boat, on the design of a triangular saloon table that raises and lowers on a hydraulic cylinder. Form plus function equals fun.

In case you think cruisers have all the fun, however, consider lifetime sailor and addicted IMS and PHRF racer John Yeigh, who, with his wife, Karen, spends most of his time aboard their S2 10.3 winning Chesapeake Bay championships. Yeigh discovered that the tubular foam lifeline pads that are sold commercially disintegrate in a relatively short time. So he invented his own and had a sailmaker cover them with canvas at reasonable cost in the off-season. Not only is Yeigh's back spared after long stints of watching sail trim from the helm, but his boat looks great because the canvas matches the sail covers.

Fun is coming up with ingenious tricks for making daily living tidier, more comfortable, and more enjoyable. Fun is having a party, sailing well, and being proud of your boat. But best of all, fun means you're a kid again.

Umbrella Sailing

It must be at least a half-mile from your mooring to your dinghy dock. You've rowed the tender in twice today. Is there a breeze? Take your umbrella, writes Charles Rice of Goldsboro, North Carolina.

For several years he has carried a golf umbrella in his dinghy. "When the wind is fair, it makes a fine spinnaker/reacher, secured by a light line and a rolling hitch on its handle. Chances are you'll have a fair breeze at least one way. You can tether your umbrella handle, steer with an oar or paddle, and prepare to receive queries and compliments. The dome shape creates some lift, so a degree of close-reaching is possible. The umbrella can rest against the dinghy gunwale, though you should raise it periodically to clear the blind spot.

"The smaller the tender, the better the sail area-to-displacement ratio. My golf umbrella has almost 20 square feet of sail area—a big boost to a small dink with tiny oars. For a larger inflatable, a beach umbrella provides 28 or more square feet."

Stereo Alternative

Richard J. Raburn, owner of *Mandarin*, a 1948 S&S Pioneer Class ocean racer, has an interesting alternative to an expensive stereo system.

He replaced a defunct car stereo unit, suffering from condensation formed inside his sloop's aluminum hull, with a 30-watt-per-channel booster amp, and a portable disc player he was already using in his car and with his home stereo.

By adding the right size plug-in terminals to his boat's existing speaker cables he was able to connect the cables to the new booster amp and can now simply plug in his portable CD deck when the desire for music arises.

This alternative offers two advantages: First, the player leaves the boat, limiting salt air and condensation damage as well as eliminating the threat of theft; and second, many people already have a portable disk or cassette player for auto/home use.

The installation required an afternoon's work and an expenditure of less than $100, not including speakers.

Sailboard Rack

Dan Welch of Orange, California, has found that car roof-rack systems can be creatively adapted to boats for those who want to bring their sailboard along on a cruise. He suggests that the best location for the board itself is out of the way on the foredeck. Lay the board against the lifelines with the skeg (fin) forward and outboard, or remove the skeg altogether. Pad the stanchions well (car roof-rack pads are ideal) and use top-quality adjustable straps, such as Thule, Terzo, or Yakima (roof-rack straps are available at most sporting-goods stores). It's also a good idea to cover the board with a simple canvas board bag for sun protection.

As for the board's mast, just what do you do with a 14-foot fiberglass vaulting pole? Your best bet is to buy a two-piece spar. If you do have a one-piece mast, however, stow it like a spinnaker pole at the mast or, as Welch prefers, on car-rack pole holders. Attach the holders to stanchions to secure the mast. The boom may be stored on deck strapped to the board, but it is generally preferable to disassemble it and store it below.

Sails should always be stored below. "I cringe when I see $200 to $600 sails wrapped around the mast or lying in the scuppers," says Welch. "The sun and salt will eat through a Dacron or Mylar sail faster than you can write a big check for a new one." Instead, loosen the battens, roll the sail, bag it, and stow it below. Be ready to stow all gear below when heavy weather threatens.

Bird Whacker

Captain Dean Coe copes with cormorants and other avian pests intent upon fertilizing the foredeck of his sloop with a trick lacking in aesthetics but brimming with positive effect.

fastened to his jib-halyard shackle, forming a "T." He shackles a downhaul line to the bottom loop, then raises the halyard to about 10 inches above the spreaders. The downhaul is fastened to the bow pulpit, leaving enough slack so that it can swing but the shackle will not come within three or four inches of the mast. The hose swings freely from side to side in an unpredictable pattern, making it

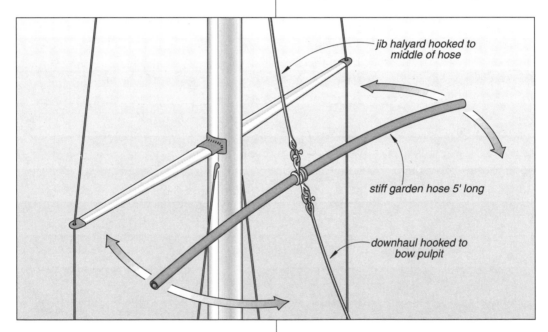

jib halyard hooked to middle of hose

stiff garden hose 5' long

downhaul hooked to bow pulpit

His bird whacker is a five-foot piece of stiff garden hose clamped with two loops lashed at its midpoint. The top loop is

impossible for the bird to maintain its perch without getting hit. The slightest breeze, wave action, or boat wake sets the

Seagull Chaser

Hank Parisi of San Marcos, California, has an idea for sailors who are tired of seeing their neat and nicely tucked mainsail covers spotted and stained with seagull "calling cards." He says, "Simply tie a piece of line around your mast and stretch it out the length of your boom, securing it to the topping lift or backstay. Keep it as parallel to the boom as possible, about 2 to 4 inches above the mainsail cover. The line itself is too unstable to allow gulls to land on it, and it forms a suitable obstacle to keep them from perching on your boom."

Happier Birds, Clean Deck

Bert Jackson of Marathon, Florida, has an idea for how to keep the decks clean. Pelicans and other sea birds used to sit on the pulpit of his son-in-law's CSY 37. "I finally solved the problem by actually providing the birds with a more

2x4 tied to bow pulpit

comfortable resting place: a 2x4 board, approximately 6 feet long, tied athwartships to the top horizontal rung of the pulpit, and extending out equally to port and starboard." The birds much prefer to land on the board, hence, all that "mess" goes overboard.

Clean Cats Afloat

Norma de Beer, who cruises on *Slipaway*, describes the problems faced by those who have a pet cat on board: "Get into a rough sea and over goes the sandbox, sand everywhere. Guests on board; oops, sand everywhere. Then there's the smell."

any urine goes straight through, leaving the cat's paws dry, and any droppings remain on top to be thrown out. If you attach a line to the container, it can be dropped overboard and rinsed out.

"A cat that is used to sand may need to have the sand gradually reduced while it gets used to the fishing line being in the sand," Norma adds. "Young kittens should be taught to go on a newspaper. The paper should then be put on top of

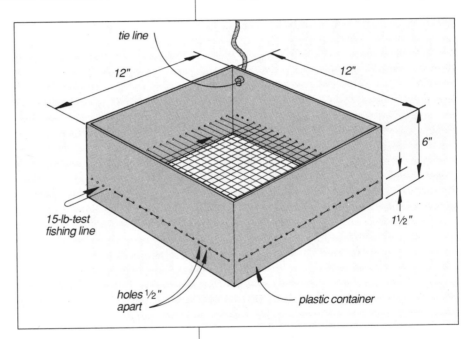

She solved the problem by making a spill-proof, smell-proof litter box with a plastic container, approximately 1 foot square and 6 inches deep. She used a hot needle to make holes ½-inch apart and 1½-inches up from the bottom of the container. Fishing line threaded back and forth across the inside bottom of the container makes a tennis racket–like surface. The cat sits on the fishing line;

the line in the box and made smaller each time until the kitten is using just the fishing line."

For times in port, a second box, with the bottom cut out, could be fixed to the toerail so it hangs outboard. This could provide your cat an open-air toilet area and free you from having to empty the container as frequently.

Lifeline Covers

The foam lifeline covers sold in marine stores are relatively expensive; after a season or two in the sun, they begin to disintegrate and look tattered. John Yeigh, who races and cruises the Chesapeake on an S2 10.3, has a solution.

He bought inexpensive pipe insulation from a hardware store (99 cents for a 6-foot length). He then had a sailmaker sew tubes of cloth to fit over the insulation. The tubes match the boat's sail covers and cost only $8 each because they were ordered during the sailmaker's off-season. John's lifeline covers are now two years old and should last several more. They make lounging against the lifelines more comfortable, and they actually dress up the boat.

Comfort on the Rail

Larry Stephenson has received great reviews since replacing the lifeline in his cockpit with straps made primarily from 2-inch-wide webbing. Two pieces of webbing are sewn together with a length of batten sandwiched inside. The ends are overlapped and sewn closed around large D-rings. The end result gives you a nice wide area on which to lean that won't wrinkle or twist and gives up little of the strength necessary for safety. Now, whether on the leeward rail or just leaning back and relaxing, the safety line doesn't detract from comfort on the rail.

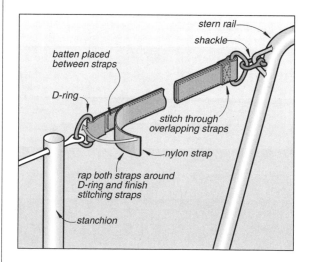

stern rail

shackle

batten placed between straps

D-ring

stitch through overlapping straps

nylon strap

rap both straps around D-ring and finish stitching straps

stanchion

Boom Support

Philippe Von Hemert of Philadelphia, Pennsylvania, has a good, simple idea for small-boat owners who do not want to install a permanent boom gallows but wish they could sometimes position the boom off center while in port.

To save guests from hitting their heads as they climbed out the companionway on *Chimera*, his 26-foot gaff-rigged sloop, Philippe designed and built an asymmetrical scissors boom support. He used ¾-dimension (1¼-inch) oak and cut the starboard leg of the scissors shorter than the port. As the companionway is about 8 inches off center to port and his boom rests 8 inches off center to starboard on the new improved scissors, the companionway is virtually clear of obstructions. Reversing the support would work, too.

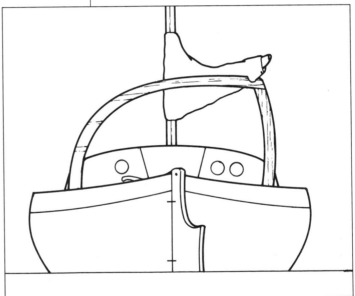

Cockpit Table

Like many of those who choose tiller steering, Robert Miner of Strongsville, Ohio, wished he could figure out a way to have a simple-to-mount cockpit table. Without a wheel pedestal to which one end of the table can be attached, this presents a problem. Miner designed his own solution, one that shows some careful thought.

He writes: "The table has three legs, which are hinged beneath the tabletop. The front leg flairs at the top to nearly half the width of the table, giving strength to the hinged joints—that is, the single central leg on the forward end provides knee room for easy seating access and folds between the two legs on the aft end for storage. The two aft legs drop into tight-fitting U-shaped brackets mounted high on the forward face of the lazaret

or helmsman's seat. A pin at the bottom of the forward leg drops into a socket in the cockpit sole. This makes the table quite stable, though some day I'll probably add pins to the bottoms of the aft legs to prevent the little bit of forward movement that is possible there.

"The folded table is 2 inches thick and stores against the empty bulkhead in our head. It drops into brackets at the bottom corner and is dogged down near the top. Velcro patches hold the legs against the bottom of the table when I am carrying it through the boat."

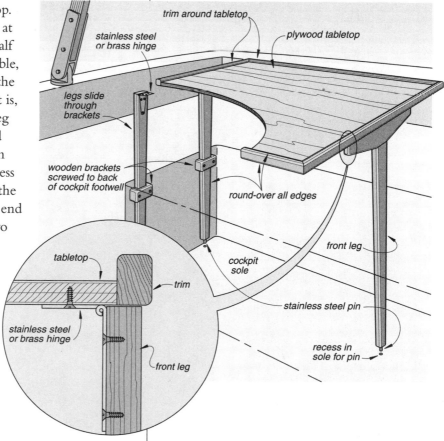

trim around tabletop

plywood tabletop

stainless steel or brass hinge

legs slide through brackets

wooden brackets screwed to back of cockpit footwell

round-over all edges

tabletop

trim

stainless steel or brass hinge

front leg

cockpit sole

front leg

stainless steel pin

recess in sole for pin

Custom-Fitted Cockpit Drink Holder

An inexpensive, custom-fitted removable holder for canned drinks was suggested by Jane Piereth of San Rafael, California. To make it, she writes, "Trace the shape of the bottom five inches of your companionway board onto a piece of plywood. Cut out the shape and fasten it to a four-hole teak drink holder (available from marine stores and catalogues) by drilling and screwing from behind. No holes need to be drilled in the boat, and the holder is low, so it is easy to step over when you use the companionway. If you leave a half-inch of plywood above the teak holder, it will take the brunt of the abuse if someone does step on it. When the holder is not in use, I stow it upside down at the head of a quarterberth."

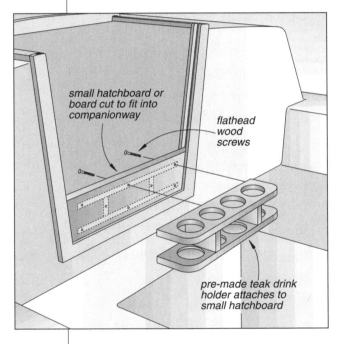

small hatchboard or board cut to fit into companionway

flathead wood screws

pre-made teak drink holder attaches to small hatchboard

Instant Cockpit Table

Natalie and Al Levy of Chicago, Illinois, have found that the commodious cockpit often found on small cruisers becomes the rendezvous for après-sail gatherings. They write: "We were looking for a place to set food and drink when we discovered, quite by accident, that our Ensign's cabin doors readily slide off their hinges and neatly span the distance between the cockpit seats at approximately midpoint. Even with six or eight people aboard, everyone is within arm's length of 'chow.' This ever-present, readily stowable cockpit table may be an undiscovered treasure on many other boats as well."

The Pardeys point out that the hinges on the Levy's boat were designed so the doors could be lifted off. If yours are not, the Murry snap-apart hinge (from Jamestown Distributors, 28 Narragansett, Jamestown, Rhode Island 02835) works for any application—like companionway ladders, doors, or lids—where you need a hinge but also want to remove the hinged item.

Instant Ice

Terry O'Brien and Shelley Parsons left Portland, Oregon, aboard their 36-foot cutter, *Whisper*, with a small 12-volt refrigerator aboard, but no way to make ice cubes.

Shelley rectified this situation by filling sealable (Ziploc-type) bags half full of water and hanging them with wooden

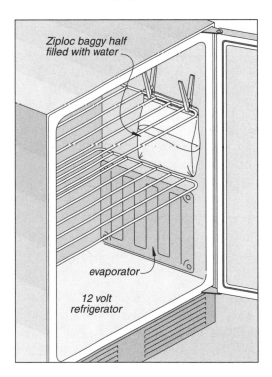

Ziploc baggy half filled with water

evaporator

12 volt refrigerator

clothes pins over the evaporator plate in the refrigerator. Terry writes: "*Voilà!* Ice! Just the right amount to enjoy with an adult beverage as we watch the sun set in the beautiful Caribbean."

Ice for Coffee?

Marvin Reynolds of Holliston, Massachusetts, and his wife, Juli Ann, both enjoy a cup of good coffee aboard their Baba 35, *Anastasia*. However, the water from their annually flushed water tanks did not give them the taste they desired.

The solution was to freeze two half-gallon containers of drinking water and use these for "ice" for the weekend. Having left one partially frozen container

ice box

plastic containers for drinking water

in the ice box, they returned the following weekend to thawed drinking water, perfect for making coffee. During the week they refroze the second container, which then provided cooling for the next trip to the boat and became the "ice" in the ice box. However, Marvin does write that "some containers can be frozen without cracking, others cannot. We learned it was always best to drain off a glass or two before freezing."

No-Effort Potato Rinsing

Carl Frostell of Djursholm, Sweden, says, "People laugh—but only once—when they see me towing a net bag full of potatoes." The fact is that the potatoes in the bag roll and scrape themselves very clean in a few minutes. The net bag is made of rather coarse cotton twine, approximately the size of an ordinary shopping bag, and has a long line to close it on top and to tow by.

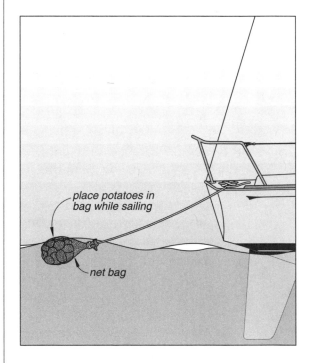

place potatoes in bag while sailing

net bag

Utensil and Plate Box

John M. Ash of Chebeague Island, Maine, has devised a handy, portable galley storage box. "I designed the box for my J/24 because I wanted to be able to offload cruising gear easily to lighten the boat for racing," says Ash.

He measured his utensils and plates to determine the size and shape each bin would have to be to hold everything without rattling. For the ends of the box he used ¾-inch mahogany with grooves in the front and back sections to hold the lighter plywood sides securely. Before he assembled the box, he cut an insert out of mahogany to separate the different sections. He attached the insert to one side of the box with wood screws and then assembled the rest of the box around it. The front compartment is large enough to accommodate dinner plates. He wedges spatulas and serving spoons around the plates to keep them secure.

"I now own a Sabre 38 and have found that the utensil box fits perfectly just inside the aft cabin. It's held in place with a screw eye and an L-hook on the bulkhead. The box is easily accessible from the galley and is a labor saver at commissioning and decommissioning times."

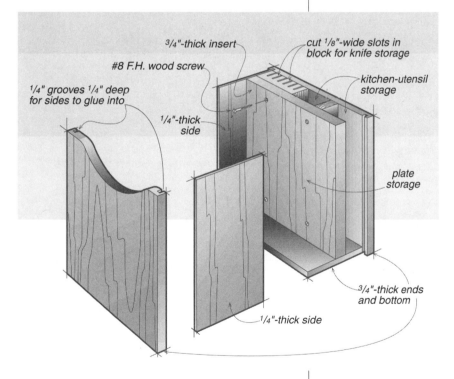

³/₄"-thick insert

#8 F.H. wood screw

cut ¹/₈"-wide slots in block for knife storage

¼" grooves ¼" deep for sides to glue into

kitchen-utensil storage

¼"-thick side

plate storage

³/₄"-thick ends and bottom

¼"-thick side

Add Counter Space

Jim Peters of Bethesda, Maryland, finds the galley workspace aboard his Catalina 27, *Windsong*, very limited. His solution is a sink-top cutting board that provides additional counter space for preparing food and remains secure even while under way.

Make or buy a cutting board that is large enough to cover the sink opening and just overlap the rim of the sink on all sides. Trim it to this size if necessary. On the underside of the cutting board, center another piece of wood that has been cut to fit the sink opening snugly, and secure the two together with stainless-steel wood screws. With the board in place, you have additional stable counter space for galley work in any conditions.

Hide-a-Compass

Lin and Larry Pardey found a useful and relatively simple way to hide the back of *Taleisin*'s compass, which sticks through into the cabin in a very conspicuous place. Larry built a simple mitered, deep-sided frame out of teak and attached it to the cabin back with hinges. A colonial latch keeps the frame closed, yet allows quick access to the compass back and frame interior. They had nonglare glass cut to fit the frame. To add variety to *Taleisin*'s interior, they made five mat boards of different colors to fit the frame (they store them inside it); now they can display a favorite photograph or sketch and change the picture from time to time.

Book Holder

Emil Gaynor of Camarillo, California, contributed this interesting solution for keeping books in place on their shelves. As he says, "There have been many schemes for holding books on a shelf; most are poor." His solution: "A piece of sail track mounted to the back of the bookshelf, a slide with a length of ³⁄₁₆-inch or ¼-inch braid, and a jam or tube cleat. This allows quick adjustment and easy removal of books with no spills or flopovers."

If you are building new shelves, the track could be made from a small piece of plate (brass or aluminum) drilled with two holes and a rabbet. This would eliminate the need for the sail track and would work just the same as Emil's slide.

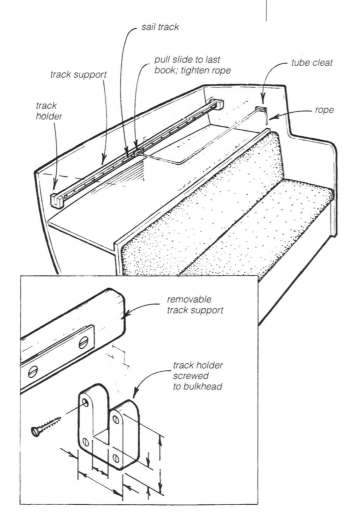

sail track

track support

pull slide to last book; tighten rope

track holder

tube cleat

rope

removable track support

track holder screwed to bulkhead

Handy Storage

Judith and Anthony Kaczor, aboard *Therapy,* found storage of small items to be a problem. Their solution was to hang two conventional shoe holders (the cloth/plastic kind that can be held up by two to three small hooks at the top and can be found in discount department stores).

This clutter organizer stores lots of items such as boat tape, cleaners, sponges, utensils, keys, wallets, registrations, licenses, sail ties, and even holds open soda cans upright. If the shoe holders are too long to fit in the area where you want them to hang, just cut off the excess.

"We installed one with two rows against the hull in our cabin area and one with four rows in the space under our cockpit."

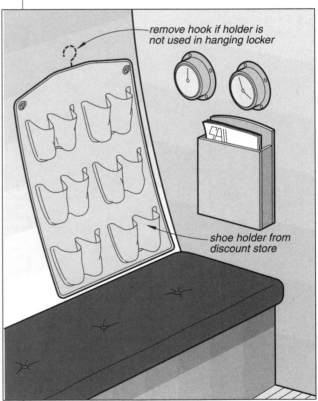

remove hook if holder is
not used in hanging locker

shoe holder from
discount store

Eyeglass Holder

Vincent O'Hara, who sails aboard *Irish Lady*, keeps his eyeglasses from falling overboard with some salty ropework. "Having lost glasses to a whipping line and the ever hungry ocean, and not wanting to look like a Down East dowager, I used the outer core of a short length of braided line, whipped the ends onto the arms of the glasses, and ended up with a very functional, neat, and nautical keeper.

"The glasses can be lowered to your chest or lifted to your head when you're below. The keeper assures that they are rarely misplaced, stepped on, or sat upon. There's a wide variety of colors and textures from which to choose, and the clean white hollow core can be saved for formal weddings."

Paper-Roll Keeper

Doug Ward of Providence, Rhode Island, owner of the Cal 229 *Remedy II*, has a simple solution for toilet paper and paper towels that unroll into a mess with the boat's motion while under way. In order to keep rolled paper in place, Doug hangs a piece of light chain over the top of each roll. The weight of the chain exerts just enough pressure to keep the rolls from unraveling.

Drying Line

Wet socks and other damp gear can alter belowdecks ambiance. Ed and Fran Lormand of Clarkston, Georgia, hang a drying line under the edge of the dinette table on the side away from the settee and people's knees. They secure a piece of nylon cord attached to a stainless-steel screw at each outside corner, snug to the bottom of the table. "For over fifteen years, including two transatlantic passages and six liveaboard summers, our drying line has worked beautifully for everything from dishcloths to socks." In the deluxe version, Ed and Fran added a piece of shock cord to eliminate line sag.

Porthole Curtains

Kim Mell and Kim Christian of Winslow, Washington, write: "After moving to our present mooring, we found that we needed to cover our portholes to have some degree of privacy. We use embroidery rings, available at most sewing stores, as removable 'curtains.' We choose material to match the area or mood, tighten it into the hardwood ring, and trim off the excess. We then screw in a single brass hook just above the port and place the frame on the hook."

V-Berth Sheets

"Keeping the V-berth shipshape and our toes covered was a constant problem on our boat, *Sweetwater*," writes Celestine Fisher of Boynton Beach, Florida. She found an inexpensive and simple way to solve the problem. She selected sheets and blankets slightly wider than the widest part of the V-berth. She folded the sheet lengthwise and sewed the bottom. She then unfolded the sheet and a V-shaped pocket was formed. The V of the berth cushions fits this pocket so you can pull the sheet tightly as you tuck it in around the sides and head of the bunk. Celestine even takes thread and needle along and does this by hand on charter boats.

Index

If you enjoyed *SAIL's Things That Work*, you may be interested in these books from the International Marine library.

Boatowner's Mechanical and Electrical Manual: How to Maintain, Repair, and Improve Your Boat's Essential Systems
Nigel Calder

Destined to be a highly trusted, grease-encrusted companion aboard boats of all types for many years to come. Includes chapters on engines, electrical systems, electronics, generator sets, solar panels, wind and water generators, transmissions, refrigeration and air conditioning, disposal systems, and much, much more.

"This book should be standard equipment with every boat."—*SAIL*

Hardbound, 544 pages, 300 photos, 300 illustrations, $39.95. Order No. 60128H

Boatowner's Energy Planner: How to Make and Manage Electrical Energy on Board
Kevin and Nan Jeffrey

A detailed exploration of onboard energy systems, including marine alternators, portable generators, solar panels, wind and water generators, battery management, AC shore-power hookups, and system controls and accessories for both DC and AC electrical service, with just enough theory to make all the options crystal clear.

"A valuable addition to any boat maintenance library."—*Offshore*

Paperbound, 288 pages, 77 illustrations, $21.95. Order No. 60234P

The Complete Canvasworker's Guide: How to
Outfit Your Boat with Fabric, Second Edition
Jim Grant

A thorough, step-by-step guide to making all common items of fabric boat gear, including boat covers, bags, sail covers, bosun's chairs, cushions, dodgers, bimini tops, flags, hatch covers, and much more. This new edition is larger by half than the universally praised first edition.

Paperbound, 192 pages, 373 illustrations, $19.95. Order No. 60323P

The Rigger's Locker: Tools and Techniques for
Modern and Traditional Rigging
Brion Toss
Illustrated by Robert Shetterly

An all-new collection of useful ideas, undeservedly obscure knots and splices, and tips on everything from working safely aloft to splicing wire, splicing braided rope, splicing rope to chain, rigging self-tending headsails, and even preventing the eternally irritating problem of keeping that drawstring from disappearing into the waistband of your sweatpants.

Hardbound, 224 pages, 237 illustrations, $24.95. Order No. 60126H

Boat Joinery and Cabinetmaking Simplified
Fred P. Bingham

Drawing upon more than 60 years' experience as a boatbuilder, cabinetmaker, and designer, Fred Bingham has revamped his classic *Practical Yacht Joinery* to appeal to a whole new generation of boatbuilders.

"A veritable encyclopedia of techniques, tools, gadgets, and gimmicks."
—*Dolphin Book Club News*

Paperbound, 304 pages, 475 illustrations, $24.95. Order No. 60356P

Please turn over for order form.

Look for These and Other International Marine Books at Your Local Bookstore

To Order, Call Toll Free 1-800-822-8158
(outside the U.S., call 717-794-2191)

or write to International Marine, A Division of TAB Books,
Blue Ridge Summit, PA 17294-0840.

- -

Title	Product No.	Quantity	Price

Subtotal: $_____

Postage and Handling
($3.00 in U.S., $5.00 outside U.S.): $_____

Add applicable state and local sales tax: $_____

TOTAL: $_____

❑ Check or money order made payable to TAB Books

Charge my ❑ VISA ❑ MasterCard ❑ American Express

Acct. No. _____ Exp. _____

Signature: _____

Name: _____

Address: _____

City: _____

State: _____ Zip: _____

International Marine catalog free with purchase; otherwise send $1.00 in check or
money order and receive $1.00 credit on your next purchase.

Orders outside U.S. must pay with international
money order in U.S. dollars.

If for any reason you are not satisfied with the book(s) you order, simply return it (them)
within 15 days and receive a full refund.